HOW TO PLACE THE
SUCCESSFUL
SALES
AND
PROSPECTING
CALL

ART SOBCZAK

How to Place the Successful Sales and Prospecting Call

Published By:

Business By Phone Inc.
(480)699-0958
E-mail Arts@BusinessByPhone.com
www.BusinessByPhone.com

ISBN: 978-1-881081-01-2

Cover design http://fiverr.com/visualarts
Interior design by Adina Cucicov

Table of Contents

About Art Sobczak

Since 1983, Art Sobczak, President of Business By Phone Inc., has specialized in one area only: authoring, designing and delivering content-rich training programs and resources that business-to-business salespeople—both inside and outside—begin showing results from the very next time they get on the phone. Audiences, customers, and readers love his "down-to-earth," entertaining style, and low-pressure, easy-to-use, customer oriented ideas and techniques.

He works with thousands of sales reps each year helping them get more business by phone. Art provides real world, how-to ideas and techniques that help salespeople use the phone more effectively to prospect, sell, and service, without morale-killing "rejection."

In 2012 Art received the Lifetime Achievement Award from the American Association of Inside Sales Professionals for his contribution to the profession. In 2015, once again he was named one of the Top 50 Sales and Marketing Influencers, by Top Sales World.

Using the phone in sales is only difficult for people who use outdated, salesy, manipulative tactics, or for those who aren't quite sure what to do, or aren't confident in their abilities. Art's audiences always comment how he simplifies the sales process, making it easily adaptable for anyone with the right attitude.

Since 1984 Art has written and published the how-to tips newsletter, The Smart Calling Report, and for over 16 years, his weekly email tips newsletter.

Art is a prolific producer of learning resources on selling by phone. His newest book, *"Smart Calling"—How to Take the Fear, Failure, and Rejection Out of Cold Calling,"* hit Number One in the Sales and Marketing category on amazon.com on its very first day of release, and was named Top Sales Book of 2010 by Top Sales Awards. The Second Edition was released in 2013. And perhaps the most notable testament to the book's effectiveness, it is on the list of amazon.com's Top 20 most highly rated sales books of **all time**.

He holds the popular Smart Calling College two-day public training seminars nationwide, and now online. He also customizes the program for on-site, in-house delivery. Art also delivers how-to programs on effective inside sales and cold calling ranging from one-hour to several days.

He has produced and delivered over 1500 training sessions over the past 33 years for companies and associations in virtually all business-to-business industries.

His speaking and training reputation has been built as someone who knows what works and what doesn't in sales because he's done it (corporate inside sales and management positions with AT&T Long Lines and American Express in the early 80's), and still does it.

He also conducts extensive research to customize his programs, listening to recordings of actual sales calls of client reps in order to learn the language of the industry, company, and strengths and weaknesses of sales reps and strategies.

Contact Art personally at (480)699-0958,
or SmartCalling@Gmail.com.

1 It Can And IS– STILL–Being Done By Phone

When I wrote and released the first edition of this book in 2006, I had been in the inside sales business for 23 years. During that time many many changes had taken place in business and technology.

In the 10 years since I first released this book, it is mind-boggling to think how many MORE changes have happened than in those initial 23 years.

However, some things have remained the same. The phone still is one of your most valuable sales tools.

Despite what some gurus say—who likely want to sell you the social media and "the phone is dead" training programs they are peddling—the phone is STILL the second most effective way to communicate and sell. Second only to face-to-face.

Oh sure, it is harder than ever to get through to and create interest with buyers in our crazy-busy society. What that means is that YOU need to be more interesting with your messaging and approach.

Buyers are still talking to salespeople. The savvy ones. That's who you want to be.

I'm assuming you aren't buying into the garbage perpetuated by the "calling is dead" crowd. Good for you, because you are right.

I know as a fact that using the phone in prospecting and sales works. I prove it. My clients prove it. And hundreds of thousands of salespeople also prove it every day.

As Jeb Blount writes in his latest book, *"Fanatical Prospecting,"*

> *"We have stats on phone prospecting going back to the early 1990s, and we are seeing clear trends that contact rates via phone have actually risen by around 5 percentage points."*

But, in order to be successful you need to do and say the right things, and avoid what is likely to cause resistance.

In this book I'll show you the components of professional prospecting and sales telephone calls.

I'll show you what to say, why to say it, what to avoid, and how to do it. It doesn't matter if your end goal is to set an appointment, get someone to a webinar, or make a sale, the same process applies.

It doesn't matter if you are placing an initial call to a prospect you don't know, a follow-up call to someone who is in a multi-step complicated longer-term sales cycle, or a regular account maintenance call to a regular customer. The same process applies.

It' a simple process, really.

But it IS a process. There are steps to follow with a purpose for each. There are things to do and say, and to avoid that cause resistance.

Don't get too worried though. It shouldn't be, and isn't salesy or gimmicky.

When you follow my process and apply it to what you do and sell, you'll see how conversational and natural it is. That's how buyers want to be approached and spoken to, and I'm assuming that's how you'd prefer to sell and prospect.

Mostly it's common sense.

But, in my over 33 years of experience as a salesperson, manager, author, trainer, speaker, and "guru" (I hate that word) I can tell you common sense isn't all that common, or practiced.

In fact, I see many of the same mistakes being made today as I did 10, 20 and 30 years ago. And I see many more new ones as a result of misusing and abusing "geeknology." It's job security for me, but for those making the mistakes it's sales frustration and failure.

In this book I'll give you the simple step-by-step process for the successful call.

It's the same process I cover in my Smart Calling College training workshops (SmartCallingCollege.com), and my in-house customized sales programs for clients, of which I've done over 1700 of for companies in virtually every industry.

Will you become a wealthy superstar sales pro by simply reading this book?

No.

Lots of people *read* things evey day. And they probably want things like success and more money. But they fail.

Because they don't DO anything with it. Don't let that be you.

All I can promise you is that this stuff flat out works. I know it because I use it myself. Have for years. I've made all of the mistakes also. And I've sold millions of dollars worth of my own services.

And clients and customers tell me how much they've made, and what they've saved and avoided in terms of not getting the resistance, "rejection', and avoidance they were used to.

This book gives you a proven process, methods, tips, and word-for-word messaging you will be able to use to show success on your very next calls.

Will you get everything you need here to be tremendously successful? Well, let's get real here. The top professionals in every field got there through hard work, sustained learning and practice, and an insatiable desire to succeed.

I am giving you a proven process along with word-for-word messaging and techniques for each part of the call, along with how to keep your attitude high when doing it. You have the blueprint for adapting it and implementing it. Use it and you will have success. Where you really want to go with your skills and sales is up to you.

IF you do want to reach the highest levels of success and income, you'll need to continue mastering and practicing each step of the process we cover here. There are thousands of books, learning programs, and articles on all aspects of sales. The most succssful reps constantly are using them and getting better.

I have plenty of other resources to help you get there as well.

For now you'll need to supply the attitude and action.

Deal?

Master the Phone and You Will Master Sales

Again, I'm assuming you're reading this because you have bought into the fact that the better you are on the phone, the better you are in sales. Period.

Something I have heard my entire career—and it exasperates me because it's not true, especially today—is,

> *"You can only use the phone to set appointments. You can't sell (fill in the blank) _____ by phone. It's a complex, multiple call sales process."*

Someone correct me if I'm wrong, but if it's being done now, that means it's possible, right?

But, the fact is, if you're not using the phone as an integral part of your sales process, regardless of what you sell and the complexity of your sale, you're probably not as efficient or effective as you could be.

The Truths of Sales Communication

Here's my take on the issue:

1. **Sales is a** *process* where we use several methods of communication in order to achieve our objective: the sale and continuing relationship.

2. **Face-to-face selling** is the most effective way to sell because we're able to use all methods of communication; on the phone we don't have the visual element.

3. **Face-to-face selling** is by far the most costly way to sell.

4. **Many face-to-face visits** are a waste of time, whereby the same result could have been achieved by phone more quickly and less expensively. (And I haven't even begun to take into account all of the time and money spent getting to and from the meeting.)

5. **About 5%-30%** of a face-to-face call is spent on business, 70%-95% on small talk and extraneous matters. Inverse those numbers when applied to phone calls.

6. **Most face-to-face sales reps** could increase their sales by cutting their number of visits and increasing their number and quality of telephone calls, by moving the sales process closer to the end objective on the phone, so that by the time they meet with someone, they've ensured they have someone who is qualified, interested, has authority, has money, and has an immediate need.

7. **Many prospects and customers** would rather not see a salesperson; it takes too much time to get down to business.

8. **Some prospects and customers** DO sometimes demand and prefer to see salespeople, in certain buying situations (not as many as outside sales reps like to think, though).

9. **For every sales rep or manager** who says, *"You can't sell our product/ service by phone,"* there is someone already doing it. Typically I hear this statement from someone whose job is being threatened by an inside sales department, or someone not comfortable with their own phone skills. Conversely, the wealthiest and most successful reps I know are masters at using the phone **and** at face-to-face presentations.

10. **The Internet levels the playing field between inside and outside sales.** With screen sharing, webinars, webcams, web demos, the ability to transfer information instantly, and more, almost everything that needs to take place during a sales transaction can be done remotely.

11. **Social Media has not, and will not replace personal sales.** All forms of social media are tools. They are complements to actually speaking with humans. Those that believe otherwise grow poor and depressed as they hope and wish customers will contact them, ready to buy.

Handling Complex, Multiple Call Sales By Phone

Anyone who has a predetermined "leaping off point" regarding how far they'll take the relationship by phone, or how far they'll take the initial phone call (*"We only want to introduce ourselves and send out information the first call."*) is living by a self-imposed limitation that is based on false assumptions.

Here's my advice to anyone who believes this theory: Take every phone call as far as you possibly can.

Makes sense, doesn't it?

Ending a call prematurely wastes an opportunity with a captive listener you've worked hard to get to, and is interested in what you're saying. Why let him cool down considerably, meaning you have to work just as hard to bring his emotional temperature back to this point and beyond on the next contact?

Plus, one of the biggest complaints I hear from salespeople is how tough it is to reach a decisiion maker. Why in the world would we want to get off the call quickly once we ultimately get through? Crazy.

Don't follow a process that states, *"On the first call we send out a brochure. On the second we collect information. On the third we make a presentation . . ."*

What hogwash that is! Instead, establish a model that outlines the steps that must be taken and criteria met in order for someone to buy—not the number of calls it takes.

For example, a simple example scenario would be:

Stage One: qualify according to potential need, and decision-making authority.

Stage Two: Question further to identify specific problems, pains, and embellish them.

Stage Three: Present possible solutions, web demo, and get agreement on applicability and money.

Stage Four: Commitment to purchase.

Stage Five: Signed purchase agreement, credit card, or check in hand.

This process, depending on the situation, could take five calls, or one. If you had a predetermined notion that it has to take five calls, you're wasting time when you very well could have closed it in one or two. Plus, you could LOSE the sale with someone who wants to get it done earlier. Don't make them fit into *your* schedule of calls. Go with the flow.

Sales is sales. Period. Those who enjoy the greatest success use their time the most efficiently—mostly by phone.

Who is This Book For?

This is for the person who picks up the phone to initiate new contact with prospects, to follow-up on inquiries or previous calls in the sales process, and to call existing customers. Regardless of whether your desired outcome is an appointment or an eventual sale, the process applies.

It is focused primarily on a business-to-business consultative call, as opposed to a tightly-scripted word-for-word consumer telemarketing call (which has pretty much been killed off, thankfully, by the Do Not Call List.)

With that said, if you are calling people at home, or offering a consumer product such as real estate, insurance, investments, etc., the same process still applies if you want to use—and you should—a consultative, conversational sales approach.

And even if you are not really selling a product or service, but nevertheless attempting to persuade and get an end result, you will still be able to adapt the process. That includes fundraisers, recruiters, the person who is tasked with getting volunteers for the church event, and so on. In every case, the "sale" we refer to in the process is the end result.

The Successful Sales Telephone Call Process

So, fellow sales pro, here is the process we'll cover for every professional sales or prospecting call using the phone.

Pre-Call Planning
Pre-Decision Maker Communications
Interest-Creating Opening
Questions
Recommendation
Commitment
Setting Up the Next Action

In addition, I'll add important material on dealing with resistance and objections, and how to stay motivated in the process. And, we'll look at some examples of calls in order to illustrate my points.

As we go through these sections I suggest you don't just read them. DO them. Have a pen in hand. Take notes in this book, and on paper. The outcome of what you'll go through here is to help you sound like a smooth, polished professional, delivering just the right words to help someone else take action. In order to reach that point, you will need to read, write, recite, and practice.

Let's get started!

2 Pre-Call Planning: Steps To Take Before The Successful Call

CALL PROCESS

Pre-Call Planning
Pre-Decision Maker Communications
Interest-Creating Opening
Questions
Recommendation
Commitment
Setting Up the Next Action

Before you even *consider* picking up the phone, let's look at the steps the most successful sales reps take.

At the Start of the Day

Set Objectives for the Day. Prepare your "To Get Done" list. Include not only the important calls you need to make, but the other duties you must perform, such as proposals and handling service issues. Review your calendar for follow-up calls you've scheduled. Set aside blocks of time for your prospecting, account management calls, and whatever else you plan to get done. Then review your list, prioritize your plans and get rid of things that don't really need to be done, or delegate the ones that can be handled by someone else.

> *Best Yet:* do as much of this as you can the night before—particularly your call research—or begin thinking about it in the shower, or during the drive or ride to the office. You'll hit the ground running!

Prepare Your Area. Some reps' work spaces look like the aftermath of a tornado. Quite distracting, to be sure. Others often are caught unprepared on calls, prompting them to dig wildly through piles on a call like a dog searching for a buried bone. Think they're paying attention to what's happening on the call? Fat chance. Place all the prompts and resources you'll need during the day in front of you, and clear away the distractions. You'll be better prepared and more focused.

Prepare Your Mind. You wouldn't engage in strenuous physical activity without warming up your muscles; do the same with your mind. Be sure you possess the right attitude before you start. Clear your head of the thoughts of the jerk who cut you off on the drive in. Forget about the cranky kids who wouldn't listen to you that morning. Think positively. Ask yourself, *"What am I grateful for today?"*

Focus on what you want to accomplish. *"How can I help more people today?"*

As trite as it might seem, force yourself to smile before you begin.

Before Each Call

Do Your Online and Offline Research. I'm giving this point just a little bit of space in this book, but it's one of the most important tasks you'll perform. That's reviewing information you have about your prospect/customer, and gathering other information.

It's simple: the more you know about someone before you call, the more successful you'll be.

People don't like to talk to salespeople whom they feel are just trying to sell them something.

Think of salespeople who called you, giving you the same, droning uninspired pitch they gave to 20 people before you, and 20 after you (if they aren't hung up on first).

Contrast that with the person who says something like, "I know about you, and the needs and concerns you have, and the things you want to accomplish, and the new project you are working on and the challenges associated with it. I've worked with lots of other people like you and helped them get the results they wanted, and I might be able to help you as well."

THAT'S how we create interest, avoid sounding like a salesperson, and ultimately succeed in sales.

That also is the basis for my best-selling book, *Smart Calling—Eliminate the Fear, Failure, and Rejection from Cold Calling.* If your income and career relies on new business, and you despise "cold" calling, get Smart Calling. (Smart-Calling.com)

OK, so, where do you get information.

Websites: theirs for sure, and others.

Search Engines: search on their company, industry, contact name . . . anything that could be of value. Google has a service called News Alerts where you can enter in search terms and they will send you an email every day about any new web postings with those terms. Very nice of Google to be your own free sales assitants feeding you leads!

Your Own Database. Duh. This should be a no-brainer. But I find that in their haste to crank out calls, many reps simply don't take the time to collect this information and review it. By the way, this also means you need to be diligent at putting in notes after your calls. This becomes part of your pre-call planning for your next calls.

LinkedIn. You should be very proficient at using LinkedIn. This means having a customer-oriented profile, and not one that sounds like a resume, which is a mistake most people make. You should search-optimize your headline, and experience sections for the terms buyers would use to find someone selling what you have.

You need to constantly work on building your network, since you will find prospects in your Second Level connections. You should use LinkedIn's Advanced Search to find ideal prospects. You need to know the proper, value-based ways to connect with and message prospects.

You'll want to get involved with Groups, which are a rich source of prospects. But you'll want to engage the right way and not come across as that stalker salesperson.

Plus there are many many other nuances of LinkedIn that are beyond our scope here. Don't fret though. I do have some free and other more advanced training and resources to help you with LinkedIn:

www.LinkedInSales.Training

www.LinkedInForSalesSuccess.com

Bottom line, fellow sales rep, your credibility is perceived in direct proportion to how much your prospect or customer feels your call is about them. And you control how much effort you put into that.

Set Your Primary Objective. You wouldn't get in your car and say, "I'm going to start my car, and then just go out on the road somewhere."

No, you get in your car because you have a very specific destination in mind. And when you have a destination, then you figure out what route you need to take in order to get there. Then you follow that route. And usually you arrive.

Yet, many sales reps get on the phone with no clear, specific destination in mind. Then they end up cruising aimlessly, and not surprisingly, ending their wayward journey without a pleasing result.

Maybe you've had that feeling after a call. Where you sit there shaking your head, thinking, "What just *happened* on that call? I was all over the place."

I specifically define your Primary Objective as, *"What do I want them to DO as a result of this call, and what will I be doing?"*

Be specific. Saying, *"I'd like to call and introduce my company and see if there's any interest there,"* is weak.

Better: *"At the end of this call I would like the prospect to agree that my proposal is the one she wants to go with, and that she will take it to the committee for approval."*

Again, the emphasis must be on the DO. It must be action-oriented.

The ultimate Primary Objective is to get them to buy at the end of this call, if that is a possibility with shorter, simpler sales.

Perhaps your objective is to *"Get agreement that the customer will take your proposal to the board meeting and recommend its approval."* Maybe you want to qualify, generate interest, and get the prospect to agree to do a side-by-side comparison between his existing product and yours.

Look at these again. They all involve your prospect/customer DOING something.

And think big. One thing's for sure: if you aim low, you'll rarely hit above your target. When you aim high, you'll sometimes reach it, and on average, will achieve greater results than if you start low.

So here's your homework:

For every call you place from here on out, simply ask, *"What do I want this person to DO as a result of this call?"* That's your Primary Objective.

And when you have your end target in mind, it's much easier to plot your map, and ultimately arrive at the target.

Examples of Primary Objectives

The more specific your objective, the greater your chances of being successful. Look at these vague objectives, and their more specific alternatives.

Vague Objective: "To send them out our price list."
Stronger: "To get agreement they will compare our price list with that of their present vendor, find out how close we need to be to get a shot at the business, and to get commitment they will allow us to bid if we're within their requirements."

Vague Objective: "To introduce our company and send out information."
Stronger: "To generate interest, qualify according to my criteria, and get agreement they will read my literature, check their existing inventory, and discuss a trial order the next time we speak."

Vague Objective: "Follow up on the literature and see if they'd be interested in seeing a proposal."
Stronger: "Define specifically what criteria they will use to select their vendor, present my appropriate benefits verbally, and ask if those were in a proposal if they would lean towards picking us. If so, writing a proposal, and asking for the prospect's commitment that he will recommend us in the selection meeting."

Avoiding Rejection With Secondary Objectives

One of the biggest fears of salespeople, the one that causes call reluctance, and for some, to quit calling altogether, is the fear of rejection. You'll be happy to know that I'm going to show you how to never be rejected on a phone call. That's right. We do that with a Secondary Objective.

Set a Secondary Objective. This is what you'll accomplish, or at least attempt, at minimum on your call in case the Primary is not attained.

A *Secondary Objective* can be getting agreement that they'll accept your call in six months to discuss the results from their new vendor, and to determine if there is a possibility to work together at that time. It could be as minor as leaving them with a good feeling of your company.

As you can see, this does not involve them doing something. It's just you attempting something. Because that gives you a win.

Having a Secondary Objective is the entire key to avoiding "rejection" on calls.

You see, you are only rejected if you **think** you are. Rejection is not an experience; it's how you *define* an experience. Therefore, if can you accomplish something—anything—on a call, you've had a success of sorts. Think about what that can do for your attitude.

Rejection is not something that happens **to** you. Stuff will always happen to you. Rejection is reacting negatively to what happens to you—such as a "no"—and then calling that rejection.

On the other hand, if you can accomplish something—anything—or even attempt to accomplish something on the call, like asking about a product they are not buying from you, that could be viewed as a win for you, and you can feel good about that.

You might say that this is about semantics. And you would be right. What you say to yourself dictates your attitude and your subsequent actions.

If you end call after call with, "That sucks, I got rejected again. Here comes another one," you will hate what you're doing, you won't do it well, and eventually you'll avoid, or quit doing it.

Other Pre-Call Planning Steps

There are other steps you need to take as part of your planning. Since they are their own part of the call they have their own sections in this book:

• Prepare Your Voice Mail/Screener Strategies and Messaging
• Develop Your Opening Statement.
• Preparing Your Questioning Strategy and Plan.

Let's move on!

(Note: In every chapter I will hold you accountable to actually **do** something as a result of what we covered. These are Action Steps. I suggest you take time at the end of each section, go back and review it, give it some more thought, then write out what you will do.)

YOUR ACTION STEPS

What will you commit to DO as a result of this section?

3 Pre Decision-Maker Communications

CALL PROCESS

Pre-Call Planning
Pre-Decision Maker Communications
Interest-Creating Opening
Questions
Recommendation
Commitment
Setting Up the Next Action

In this chapter we cover the communications we have with people—and to electronics (voice mail) prior to, and sometimes instead of speaking with your intended decision maker.

Social Engineering to Smarten Up Your Calls

We've already discussed the importance of pre-call research and collecting intelligence about your prospect, the organization, and any other situational information that can help you tailor your call. Now it's time to show you how to get your very best source of real-time intelligence: social engineering.

Social engineering is simply talking to people other than your decision maker. The term has been most widely used to describe unscrupulous behavior, such as misrepresenting oneself and lying to manipulate someone to provide sensitive information. However, we use it positively and ethically to gather intelligence for our Smart Calls™.

It can be done,

- As a separate call before your first call to your prospect on initial prospecting calls, and,
- Every time you call your prospect or customer.

I find this to be the most underutilized tool available to salespeople—and the one that has the greatest possible payoff. All it requires is that you take the time to do it, develop a sense of curiosity, and cultivate some conversational questioning techniques.

Completing all of these steps may indeed grant you a revelation that many of us have had:

People are willing to give you amazing amounts of quality information if you just **ask** them.

A Computer Hacker's Story

Kevin Mitnick was one of the most notorious computer hackers in the world; and at the time of his arrest in 1995, the most wanted computer criminal in US history. After his release from prison, he wrote the book "The Art of Deception" in which he shares precisely how he pulled off many of his hacking jobs.

Mitnick claims that he compromised computers solely by using passwords and codes that he gained by social engineering; in other words, simply talking to people. Now a speaker and security consultant to corporations, Mitnick points out that the weakest link in any security system is the person holding the information. You just need to ask for it.

The Social Engineering Process

Of course, we are using social engineering in the positive sense: asking for information from people that will help other people and the organization as a whole. The social engineering process for Smart Calling™ is as follows.

Upon reaching a live voice, you:

1. **Identify yourself and your company:**

   "Hi, I'm Jason Andrews with National Systems."

This immediately shows that you are not hiding anything.

2. **Ask for help.** Perhaps one of the most magical words in the language is "Help." When you ask for help, you make a person feel needed, wanted, and important. Most people have an innate desire to serve. This appeals to that emotion.

> *"I hope you can help me ..."*
> *"I do need your help ..."*
> *"I need some assistance."*
> *"You probably work closely with Ms. Bigg, right? Great, there's some information you can probably help me with."*

Most people have an innate desire to be helpful to others in some way.

3. **Use a Justification Statement.** This is the magic key to getting cooperation. It's simply giving a reason why you are asking. It doesn't need to be complex, and in fact, should not be. Some examples are:

> *"I want to be sure that I'm talking to the right person there ..."*
> *"I'm going to be speaking with your VP of Sales, and want to be sure that I have accurate information ..."*
> *"So that I'm better prepared when I talk to your CIO, I have a few questions you probably could answer ..."*
> *"I want to make sure that what I have is something he'd show interest in. You can probably answer a few questions for me ..."*
> *"So I'm better prepared when I speak with Mr. Byer, I'd like to ask you a couple of questions first."*

This also works well on any subsequent call:

> *"There are a few things I forgot to ask Ms. Dumskin the last time we spoke..."*

The theory behind the success of Justification Statements is discussed by Dr. Robert Cialdini—widely considered as one of the foremost experts on persuasion and influence—in his classic book (which I believe should be in every serious salesperson's library) entitled *"Influence: The Psychology of Persuasion."*

Cialdini cites an experiment conducted by Harvard social psychologist Ellen Langer where students let others cut in line in front of them at the copy machine simply because they provided a reason for their request—"because I'm in rush."

Direct mail copywriters also employ this technique, often referring to it as the "Why" or the "Because."

For example, if a business is running a promotion, they know their response will increase if they give the reason for it. For example, "We need to make room for next year's new models and are clearing out the warehouse, so we are dropping prices to move the current models."

I recommend that you take the time to create your own Justification Statement—your "because" reason—and use it regularly.

4. **Ask questions.** Of course you want to ask about the basic, factual material for which you might not have information yet. This depends both on what you sell, and the level of person with whom you're speaking. In general, the higher up you go, the better the quality of information.

How Much Questioning to Do Here?

That's up to you, and the person you are speaking with. If you are at all hesitant about doing this because you fear that people don't have time to answer questions, get that out of your head right now! You will be amazed what you get if you simply ask. People are conditioned to answer questions, particularly when you follow this process.

And, you will be pleased with the payoff in terms of the sales intel you'll gather. The premise is a simple and logical one. The more you know about the buyer and his/her job, department, wants, needs . . . anything to do with what you sell . . . the better-equipped you are when you get that person on the phone.

How much information you get will depend on how much this person knows, how busy they are, and, to a degree, whether they feel they should give out information. One thing is for sure: if you don't ask for it, they certainly won't volunteer it.

Go in assuming that you can get every piece of info you need other than the ultimate decision, and work from there.

By the way, avoid saying, "Can you answer some questions for me?" Even if they know the answers, we've given them a fine way to decline. Plus, when you think about it, isn't that a question anyway? Tell them you're going to ask questions, then do it.

Smart Calling™ Exercise

1. Prepare your own script for social engineering using the process above. Be sure you have a justification statement you are comfortable with.

2. Brainstorm for the questions you will ask at all levels of an organization, and write them out. Use social engineering and you will make your prospecting calls much smarter, and successful.

Quick Prospecting Tip: Ask for the NAME of the Person who Handles What You Sell

If you don't know who you need to speak with, of course you want to get it here. HOW you ask for it does make a big difference.

If you simply said, "Yes, I need to speak with the person there responsible for your printing," what might happen? They might grant your request! Then what? If the buyer answered the phone with, "Hello," you would look like a real dufus when you sheepishly say, "Uh, hi. What's your name?"

Here's the better alternative.

> *"I'm looking for the name of the person there who is responsible for the acquisition of..."*
> *"I'd please like the name of the Vice President of Operations."*

I have heard back from reps who've used this, only to have harried operators transfer the call. No problem. An alternative that solves it:

> *"Before you transfer me, I'd like the name of the person there who handles..."*

Connect Now, or Later?

As I mentioned earlier, if you are placing your very first call to an organization you might want to collect your thoughts and research, plan, and do a separate, later call to your target.

Whether you ask to be transferred now or later depends on how quick you can compile and plug your newfound info into an opening statement and prepare your questioning. In any event, you'll be much better prepared than if you had to ask these same questions of the decision maker.

Not Gatekeepers. Not Screeners. Assistants

Personally, I avoid using the negative terms screeners and gate-keepers. And methodologies like getting past the gatekeeper, and ". . . avoid giving them information." These words and attitudes result in adversarial approaches—not a good strategy when they hold the key to the door.

The salespeople who are getting through understand that assistants are assistants to the buyer, and can provide assistance to them, the salesperson as well.

Assistants are there for a reason: to protect the decision maker's time. They do indeed get rid of salespeople. In fact, they are pros at it. They are getting rid of the self-interested salespeople who play the cat and mouse game and aren't able to communicate that they might have something of value for the buyer.

I've got files of success stories of how assistants have helped salespeople get their message to the buyer, arranged meetings, and even influenced purchases.

Bottom line, here's my main rule on working with assistants:

Treat them—and everyone you speak with—like a buyer.

That's right. There should be no going around, over, under, through, or past "screeners." Don't be evasive or use inane manipulative techniques.

Don't think you are smarter than them. They have seen every trick in the book, and have gotten rid of many salespeople more clever than you.

They don't get rid of everyone, though. Just the ones they deem as "salespeople" who don't have anything important enough for the boss.

Free Ebook On Getting Through

Instead of being redundant here with tips on dealing with assistants and getting through, take a moment and download this free 32-page ebook I have created. It's full of tips, examples, strategies and scripts for getting to buyers. I've included a number of success stories and case studies from my readers who shared the secrets of what's working for them to get through.

Download it free at
http://SmartCalling.Training/getting-through

Assistant and Voice Mail Tips to Help You Get Through

OK, you got the ebook, right? Great. Here are some additional ideas to help with assistants and voice mail.

Don't Get Lost in the Phone System Bermuda Triangle. When initially trying to locate a decision maker you've never spoken with, if you detect even the slightest bit of hesitation in an assistant's voice when they give you a name, continue questioning. Nothing is as frustrating as being shoved from one unwanting soul to another like a hot potato. Find out the title and department before you're sent there.

Ask for the Highest Level. Find the level higher than the one that typically makes the decision. This way, if you need to be referred, it's better to say that you,

> *"... were speaking with Karen at Mr. McNabb's office, and she felt that Ms. Collins would be the person I should be speaking with."*

It's important that you don't imply that Mr. McNabb said that she should buy from you; just let them know that you've come from above and your call will implicitly carry more clout.

Go to Other Departments. This also works when an operator or assistant is not authorized to give out the names of the people you're looking for. Ask for someone in sales . . . you know they're always willing to talk! Larger companies have purchasing departments that might be able to help. You might end up speaking with these people eventually, but what you really want to find out now is who uses and recommends your products. If you run into a talkative purchasing agent, you just might also learn who they're buying from, what they spend, and other goodies that can help you. Even if you do land at the polar opposite of where you need to be in a company, use something like this:

> *"I hope you can help me. I'm not in the right department, and you can probably point me in the correct direction. I'm Dale Strong with Thomas Development. I'm looking for the name of the person who handles the site selection for your franchises."*

Listen to their Entire Voice Mail Message. If you don't, you might be missing potentially useful information. I was sitting in with a sales rep listening to calls, and as soon as the voice mail answered, she hung up. I asked her to call back and listen again. On the recording she this time heard the person say that he wasn't going to be at this location for the next several days since he was at his other brand new location, and gave the phone number, and the hours he would be there! Now this rep knew nothing about the other location, but called him there, congratulated him on his expansion, and managed to close a sale right there!

Be prepared for voice mail. Don't place a call without being ready to leave a statement on voice mail. Not just any message, though. Talk about ideas that you have which may potentially help them benefit in some way, or avoid loss. Talk about a problem you've solved for another company, and mention you'd like to ask them a few questions to determine if it would work for them as well.

Sound interesting. There's something psychological about talking to voice mail that causes even the most eloquent speakers to lapse into their robot-like voice. Be yourself! Visualize the live person you are speaking to at the other end, not a passionless microchip! Practice your messages. Recite—do not read—them into your own recorder. Listen to yourself, being very critical about areas you want to improve. Focus on your inflection, putting variation in your voice to convey the moods of enthusiasm, urgency, and importance you desire to convey. Be sure your articulation is crisp, especially in pronouncing the ends of words and consonants.

Hang up if you need to. If you are not prepared, and the recording has the effect of erasing all signs of intelligence from your short-term memory, like a computer experiencing a data-zapping power surge, hang up before you say anything. Think through the message you'd like to leave. **Then** call back. Or, if their system allows it, review your message to be certain you're comfortable with it. If not, do it over.

Answer Assistants' Questions. Never try to evade an assistant's question. That's one sure way to get dumped. They simply want to determine if you have something of value. Use something like,

> *"Let me explain why I'm calling. We work with companies such as yours that do large numbers of air express shipments to help them cut down on their total bill each month, and in some cases the savings run from a few dollars to a few thousand. Whether or not we could do the same for you depends on several variables that I'd like to discuss with Mr. Holloway."*

Back Up Your Voice Mail Message With a Live One

If you do leave a lengthy voice mail message (one packed with results and benefits for the listener, of course), consider leaving a brief message with a secretary or assistant as well, referring to the voice mail message. Such as,

> *"Please tell him that I left him a detailed voice mail on how he could lower his materials costs."*

Handling Unreturned Voice Mails

Tom Mason, New Business Development Manager with Maclean Computing weighed in with a few good ideas, including one on how he handles prospects who don't return the voice mail messages he leaves them. Here is an email he sends them.

Dear Ms. Prospect,

My name is Thomas Mason, and I work for a company called Maclean Computing Ltd. On the 5th of June, I spoke to Mark and he suggested that I speak to you regarding what we do here. I have tried to contact you since, on four separate occasions. The dates for contact are the 11th of June, 20th of July, 23rd of July, and the 29th of July.

The reason for this e-mail is that I am concerned that I have done something wrong and that this is the reason why you are not returning my calls. Hence the title of my e-mail: "Advanced Apologies." If I have done something wrong I would like to find out, so I can correct it. If you would like to talk to me, please give me a call at 09-377-0840 or e-mail me at _____.

Thank you for your time.

Thomas Mason :-)

After nine months of using this, Tom gets enjoys about a 90% hit rate, which is quite good when most people would normally give up.

It's tough to sell if you can't get through. Try these ideas.

Where's The Voice Mail Example That Gets Calls Returned?

If you're looking for that one magic voice mail message that gets calls returned every time, well, yeah, so am I.

Other than lying, saying it's a personal call when it's not, claiming you're with the IRS, or otherwise being deceptive, the only way to get calls returned is to SAY SOMETHING OF INTEREST.

No tricks. No magic.

And, the great voice mail message is really the same as your great opening statement. So let's get started on that.

YOUR ACTION STEPS

What will you commit to DO as a result of this chapter?

4 Your Interest-Creating Opening Statement

CALL PROCESS
Pre-Call Planning
Pre-Decision Maker Communications
Interest-Creating Opening
Questions
Recommendation
Commitment
Setting Up the Next Action

Your opening statement, what you say in the first 10 seconds, is the key to a successful prospecting or sales call.

It's here where the prospect/customer decides if they'll listen to you and participate, or begin whisking you off the phone.

I've found that a great start in building successful openings is understanding and avoiding the mistakes that are sure to cause resistance.

Let's first review some Do's and Don'ts.

Openings to Avoid

"I'm calling to check in with you . . ." I jokingly refer to this as the "Probation Officer" approach. If you don't have something of value to offer, don't bother checking in. They've got enough people working with them and for them "checking in" in person all day long.

"Just wanted to touch base with you . . ." Ditto the above.

"Wanted to call to see if there was anything you needed . . ." Need is a matter of perception. If they perceived a need that was intense enough to take action on, they would have done something about it. It's your job to remind them of a need, to get them thinking about one they didn't even know they had, or to help them recognize that a mild need is actually more significant than they thought. Calling to "see if they have any needs" is reactive, and actually is a nuisance call if the customer doesn't feel like he gained as a result of the call. Some might vehemently argue this point, but what if every vendor they've ever purchased from called regularly, just to call? It's a waste of time.

"Calling to see if you received the email/letter/brochure/package/ catalog/price list I sent?" Is the literature going to do the selling for you? If so, why are you needed?

"Wanted to introduce my company and products to you ..." So what? They don't care about your products. They can look in a directory and find at least 10 companies selling the same thing.

"Like to set up a time to get together ..." The arrogance and ignorance of some salespeople blows me away. They think that just because they took the time to pick up the phone, they deserve 20 minutes of someone's time in person. No, we must *earn* the right to someone's time by showing them the value they could receive from us. And we must keep earning it throughout our calls (and visits).

How to Create Interest Every Time With Your Openings

Now that we've covered what immediately turns otherwise nice upstanding citizens into fire-breathing, crazed demons, let's discuss the much more pleasant alternative: interest creating, curiosity piquing utterances of brilliance that mesmerize them into clinging to your every word. (Well, that's your goal, isn't it?)

The opening is without a doubt the most critical part of your call. It's like the first section of a bridge. If it is not structurally sound and therefore crumbles, the remainder is useless.

First, there are two results you are looking for from your opening:

1. **Put them in a positive frame of mind, and,**
2. **Move them to the questioning part of the call.**

To accomplish this logistically, your opening needs to,

- identify you,
- let them know what's in it for them, and,
- get them involved.

As mentioned earlier, your goal is not to sell, or ask for a decision or appointment in the opener. That's a sure way to make them as elusive as a butterfly in a windstorm.

The Interest-Creating Prospecting Opening Statement Process

OK, let's tie things together and give you the blueprint for your successful call opening.

1. **Identify yourself and company.** *"Hi, I'm Dan Seller with EduTainment Industries..."* Pretty simple so far.

2. **Mention your connection/Smart Call intelligence.** Here's where you set yourself apart from every other salesperson. You connect with them because you are talking about them and their world.

"In speaking with your shipping manager, I understand that you're now experiencing delays on some of your time-critical shipments..."

3. **Let them know what's in it for them.** THIS IS THE MOST IMPORTANT PART! Take a few minutes and grab a large piece of paper. Answer these questions:

> *What do your prospects want most in life as it relates to your types of products and services?*
> *What do they want to avoid?*
> *How else can you help them personally?*

There you have it! The very reasons why they buy from you, and why they'll listen to you. Your answers are Possible Value Propositions (PVP's). Forget all that mumble-jumble about feature-advantage-benefit-proof etc., etc., ... people buy results.

Again, people don't buy your thing or stuff. They buy the RESULT. That goes into your PVP.

For example,

> *"Hello Ms. Sturgeon, I'm Sandy Carp with Aqua Industries. I understand that fine-tuning your bidding process is something that you've been discussing there. I'm calling today because we specialize in working with building contractors, and have a system that helps them minimize or eliminate cost overruns, while ensuring they get projects done on time..."*

Notice, that opener didn't talk about the fact they sell a software program to do that—the listener doesn't give a hoot about the product. He doesn't care about the means at this point; the end, the result, is what really matters.

Another favorite of mine that's easy and effective is,

> *"I've got a few ideas I'd like to run by you regarding how we might be able to _____."*

Then you simply fill in the blank with the answer to one of the questions you asked yourself earlier.

4. **Get them involved.** I'll repeat it again: you don't want to sell in the opening; just move them to the questioning, and have them be in a receptive, curious frame of mind when they arrive. I like to say,

> *"... and to determine if this is would be of value to you, I'd like to ask a few questions about how you're now handling your project management."*

Or, you can use phrases like,

> *"... and to determine if what we have would be worth taking a look at, I'd like to find out more about ..."*

Another is,

> *" . . . and to see if this is something you'd like to discuss further, I'd like to ask a couple of questions about how you're handling . . ."*

You'll know you've succeeded when they say, "Sure, go ahead and ask," or, "Fine, what do you want to know?"

Before you even consider delivering an opener, listen to it as if you were the person hearing it. Ask yourself if you would be truly inspired by it. If not, can it. If you don't, your listener will. The magic that moves them to the positive frame of mind is in appealing to what they want. And that's how you create interest every time.

The Follow-Up Call Opening

This is for any call that follows a previous contact. It's an easier opening to craft than most of the others since it's a continuation of the previous contact. What we want to avoid is being purely passive and saying something like, "I'm just following up on our last call . . ." or "Just wanted to be sure you got my email and wanted to see if there are any questions.

We want to be sure the follow up opening is proactive and leads us into a conversation with the prospect or customer, instead of asking a question that they can answer with, "Nope, no questions."

Here is the simple process to follow:

1. **Identify yourself and company.**

2. **Remind them of Your Previous Contact.** On your fol-low-up calls it's important to remember that your prospects are likely not doing pre-call planning like you. Therefore, you can't assume they are in the same frame of mind as you when your call arrives. Actually, you should assume they might not even remember you. Then you'll make it a point to briefly review where you left the previous conversation:

   "I'm calling to continue our conversation from last week..."
   "I'd like to pick up where we left off last Monday..."

3. **Remind them of Their Interest, and/or Agreed-To Action**

   "... where we had discussed your interest in our testing pro-gram, and you were going to review the statistics I sent you..."
   "... you had felt that our coverage would be more comprehen-sive for your facility and you were going to recommend it to your CFO..."

4. **Bring Something New to the Table and Be Proactive With Your Intentions for This Call**

   "... I'd like to go through those numbers with you and I have some additional information I believe you'll find beneficial."

Let's look at an example with all of the components:

> *"Don, it's Pat Keeler with Building Suppliers. The last time we*
> *spoke, last November, you asked me to contact you about your*
> *plans to expand into roofing supplies since you felt you could*
> *sell quite a bit to your existing customers. I've put together some*
> *ideas that have worked very profitably for other wholesalers*
> *across the country, and if I've reached you at a good time, I'd*
> *like to discuss your plans."*

Opening Rules, Ideas and Tips

Have Value Added Points (VAP's) on Every Call to Existing Accounts. If you are truly calling to keep your name in front of them, fine. It's necessary to build "mindshare." But this is only successful if they feel they received something as a result of the call. Be prepared with useful news, new ideas, information about how some of your other customers are taking fuller advantage of some of the things they are buying now, and so on.

For example,

> *"I was at a trade show last week and I thought of you..."*
> Or, *"We've just introduced something here that might be able to*
> *work in your situation, and I'd like to run it by you..."*

Be Proactive. Even if you did send literature, don't bring the call to a screeching halt by asking if they received it. Make it part of what you want to DO together on this call:

> *"I'd like to review with you the pricing options I detailed in my letter..."*

Use words like "discuss," "analyze," and "go through." And if they didn't receive your stuff or don't have it handy? No problem; the literature isn't holding you up like a crutch. Be prepared to proceed anyway.

Use Weasel Words. If you use cocky claims like *"I can show you how you can do thus and so, guaranteed,"* in your opening, people will furrow their brow, wince, and think to themselves, who *IS* this used car salesman?" Instead, ease in with words like

> *"might be able to...",*
> *"there's a possibility,"*
> *"depending on what you're doing now."*

Forget about "Making/saving them money." Look at those words again. Don't use them verbatim. Even bad salespeople say this in attempts to generate interest. I'm not implying this isn't a strong buying motivator—it's the *wording* that is ineffective. Instead, get information about them first from screeners, and then customize your opening to appeal to them personally.

"I understand you're now in the process of remodeling your order entry department. Depending on your space limitations, we might have some ways to help you keep your costs down during the design and installation stage of your office furnishings. If I caught you at a good time, I'd like to discuss your plans regarding..."

Account Management Calls: Just Introducing Yourself is NOT Adding Value

If you manage accounts, let's address your types of calls and openers.

First, let me ask. have you ever attended a business networking mixer? You know, the happy hour events where people walk around introducing themselves, hoping to make contacts that will result in referrals or business.

Oh I know they are useful for salespeople in certain types of businesses.

And perhaps the couple of events that friends have dragged me to are not representative of most, but I was amused by the ones I did visit.

I observed plenty of hungry—almost desperate—salespeople walking around, introducing themselves, feigning interest in the other person, then launching into their own pitch, stuffing their cards in the hands of everyone they could.

I'd watch people during these interactions—and experienced it myself—where after one person would leave, the other would roll her eyes and say to a companion, "Gawd, I'm glad he left."

These types of events caused me to borrow the name and attach it to a type of call: **The Networking Mixer Call**.

It's calling to say you "Just wanted to introduce yourself."

Just like at the event itself, that is not adding value on a call.

I'm talking about the sales rep who starts a call with, "I've just taken over your account/I'm new here/I'm the rep in your area and I wanted to introduce myself to you."

This type of call is very common with reps who are new to an organization, others who've just been handed inactive accounts, or accounts from a departed (and or fired) sales rep.

After introducing themselves, these callers normally continue with something about how they'll be calling on a regular basis, and if the customer ever needs anything to just call, yadda, yadda.

The callers seem nice enough when they phone, but let's get real here: what are the listeners thinking after they hear this introduction?

About the best that can be expected: "Oh, OK, thanks for calling."

And that's the response from the customers who actually ARE customers . . . those who buy on a fairly regular basis. But let's face it, most of the best accounts are quickly gobbled up by, or assigned to more experienced reps. And that leaves the marginal "accounts" that we're talking about here.

So, when these "accounts" get this networking mixer "I wanted to introduce myself"-call, the confused customers are likely thinking, "Account? I don't ever recall buying from you."

Or, "I bought from you guys once, over a year ago. I don't care who my rep is."

"I have a sales rep?"

"You're with who?"

"Oh, another new one."

I'm sure there might be some managers reading this who have instructed their reps to use the Networking Mixer Introduction, and they're feeling denial right now, trying to defend the approach, saying it's service-oriented, and all that other touchy-feely stuff.

But anyone who has actually placed these calls for a few days has likely been bloodied up enough to have realized the cold hard truth:

It wastes the listener's time.

This might come as a shock to some, but unless the customer's very business existence relies on your regular phone call, calling them with this self-serving declaration is viewed as a call that simply announces a policy YOU'VE implemented, or news at YOUR company. It's all "us" oriented. You might as well call them and say,

"I'm just calling to let you know that here at our company we've added three new people in the Accounting department, and we just resurfaced the parking lot."

Bottom line, it evokes a yawn, and a great big, "So what?"

It doesn't move you closer to your objective, which is to make a sale either on this call—or a subsequent one—and build a relationship.

So, what SHOULD you do?

First, to set things up, we'll focus on calls in a couple of categories:

The "Networking Mixer" calls . . . phoning accounts you haven't spoken with previously because they have just been assigned to you, and, regular calls to existing customers—who might be at various levels of ordering and volume frequency.

I've always said that these are some of the toughest calls to place. Because, it requires creative thinking and lots of sales pros don't want to think that hard.

Except the best sales pros. I bet you're in that group.

Lazy sales reps, or those or don't know any better, are content calling to "just touch base," or to "see if there's anything on your desk I can bid on."

These approaches are reactive, provide nothing of value, can be viewed as nuisance calls, and leave you open to being treated as a simple vendor who can be manipulated into a price war.

Calls to regular customers—those new to you, and to prospects you're clinging onto—should always contain something of value . . . something that lets the customer feel you are contributing something useful by calling.

Keep in mind that your customers are someone else's prospects. If they feel they are being taken for granted by a sales rep, or a transactional telemarketer-type who simply calls and says, "Do you have an order for me?", . . . they might eventually fall for the wooing of a competitor who is creative enough to dangle something attractive in front of them.

Also keep in mind your prospects are likely buying from someone else, and won't budge unless they see some value in what you have.

So, what to do?

Here are just a few ideas to spice up these calls to position you as a value-added resource, and not just a salesperson.

Instead of the Networking Mixer Opening

Of course you are introducing yourself, but think about WHY they would be interested in knowing you: sorry to break it to you, it's not because of the charming, witty individual that you are.

Well, maybe that will play a part later, but initially it will be because they *think* you can add some value to their world. So you must get to that quickly.

> *"Hi Pat, I'm Dale Johnson with Synergy Solutions. First, we want to thank you for your business with us the past couple of years, and I wanted to let you know that I am your point of contact whenever you need product research done and quotes so you can get answers quickly. Plus, I'll be letting you know when there are promotions that you might have interest in..."*

Begin with "YOU"

A good way to begin calls to customers is by saying something like,

> *"I was thinking of you,"*
> *"I heard some interesting information, and you immediately came to mind,"*
> *"When this news came out, I thought about you..."*

News or Trigger Events in Their World

A quick Google and LinkedIn search could bring up valuable intelligence about them or their company.

Perhaps they just won a major contract, they were featured in the news, your contact wrote an article or had an interesting LinkedIn update or Twitter post.

Change is constant, and it provides opportunities for you to add value.

Industry News

Perhaps you have some news they might not be aware of. Or, maybe they are aware of it, and you have something to help them take advantage of it. For example,

> *"Ms. Prospect, you probably are familiar with the new regulations regarding the reporting of waste disposal. We developed a way to make that less of a headache for companies in your*

situation, and I'd like to ask you a few questions to see how much of a problem you anticipate this being."

New Policies at Your Company

If you change restrictive policies that would enable you to do business with people who didn't qualify in the past, call them again.

For example, if your minimum order size has been dropped, or, you're now carrying a line that they asked for before and you didn't have it, or you've lessened credit requirements.

And with regular customers, calling with changes to their advantage is always welcome.

Promotions

Calling with the Deal of the Week is the lazy default for many salespeople.

While I don't suggest becoming known as the person who just calls with specials that your customers can cherry-pick, if you strategically call when there is a special on something you know your customer uses and might not be buying from you, that can turn into a bigger relationship.

Or, "Giving Away a Dollar Today to Get a Hundred Later" is a good strategy. I had an online service that I use call me and let me know I qualified for a better plan than the $19 or whatever I was paying monthly, and drop it to $14.

Crazy for them to do that right?

Not so much, when I consider that I've had lots of opportunities to leave them, but always remember that gesture . . . from a few years ago.

New Regime at Your Company
This can be effective for those accounts you haven't been able to break because of legitimate, real objections they had. If, for example, new management has cleaned house and improved quality, decreased errors, etc., call again, since you're now selling a new company.

Also, these can be spun into reasons for calling existing accounts.

New Capability
If you have products or services that deliver results you weren't able to before, that is always a good reason to call.

Just be sure you are positioning them in terms of results to the listener. Not, "Hey, we have a new product and we think it is great."

New You
Maybe you fell to pieces and self-destructed on a previous call. Since then you've acquired more skills and confidence.

Maybe you've come up with new ideas, or a new strategy.

Your Assignment

Of course my examples here are fairly general. You need to make them specific for your calls. And here's the best way I know for you personally to come up with great value-added reasons for calling:

Have a brainstorming session with your colleagues. Invite customer service, production, advertising, marketing, operations . . . anyone who knows your products and services. Make it a game or competition. The goal is to fill in the blank:

"The reason I'm calling is _____."

The main rule is that what goes in the blank must be perceived by the listener as something that they would view as valuable and interesting to them.

Believe me, I've done this many times with clients in training sessions and we come up with 20, 30 or more great ideas to use.

So get creative, get working, and you'll find yourself converting more of those prospects collecting dust in your follow-up file, and you'll provide more value and sell more to existing customers.

What's Missing in this Cold Call Opening Statement?

Let's end this chapter on openings by studying an example to test your understanding. Here's a cold calling opening statement suggestion I read in an online article. (It's no wonder so many people get beat up on the phone when they try stuff like this on a cold call that they think is from a supposed expert.)

> *"Hello, this is Mark Peters with Reclamation Services. We specialize in commercial recycling services, and I'd like to ask you about your company's recycling policy. Do you have just a moment for a couple of quick questions?"*

What critical component is missing?

You win the prize if you answered, **WHY** the person should take a moment to answer a couple of quick questions.

In my experience, the most common result of this type of opening is that most prospects, who of course are very busy people—AND who very well might be great prospects—see nothing of value in the call, perceive this as a salesperson wanting to pitch his service, and then quickly brush off the caller.

But what's interesting, and this continues to leave me scratching my scalp in amazement is that some people will actually answer the questions in response to an opener like this. But when they do, they still are likely bracing themselves for the sales pitch.

Sure they are still on the phone, but they're tentative, skeptical and guarded as they curtly answer the questions. Like a hostile witness on the stand in a court trial. Which is not the desirable state of mind for people you'd like to persuade.

In this book and my training programs, I'm all about crafting just the right words to form the optimal message to accomplish your objective. We want to minimize our chance of resistance and maximize our chances for success. And as I've demonstrated so many times, one or two words can make the difference.

Your opening must create the thought in their mind that you *might* be able to do something for them. This sparks their curiosity and interest, and earns the right to take some of their time, and, puts them in a more favorable frame of mind to answer your questions, since you've already hinted at the payoff for them.

Using my Smart Calling methodology we covered earlier, this missing component can very easily be added, making the example much more effective:

> *"Hi, I'm Mark Peters with Reclamation Services. I understand that you have adopted a corporate-wide green initiative and have been looking at some options. As a commercial recycling service, we specialize in helping metal service centers reduce their waste hauling expenses, get paid more for their scrap, and also help them save money on everyday paper goods. If I've reached you at a good time, I'd like to ask you about compliance guidelines you've been given to see if I could provide some information..."*

A few points that went into the creation of this:

- the caller used sales intelligence, some found on the company's own site about going "green," and also by doing "Social Engineering," which is speaking to others in the prospect's company. Therefore, he was able to instantly relate to a trigger event relevant in the prospect's world and made it about the prospect.

- the caller hinted at three concrete benefits they have provided to similar metal service centers, which would give an economic benefit in addition to helping them comply with their internal green initiative.

- the caller smoothly transitions into the questions, making it easy for the prospect to participate from a positive, receptive state of mind, like a friendly witness on the stand.

So, what type of prospect would you rather be dealing with?

YOUR ACTION STEPS

We have barely scratched the surface here about openings, but we have given you the foundation to create your own interest-creating opening message. Right now, take a prospect or customer that you will be calling, follow all of the steps up to this point (that means doing your research and social engineering call) and then plug everything in to an opening statement. Write it out, edit it, and practice it out loud.

5 Effective Questioning

CALL PROCESS

Pre-Call Planning
Pre-Decision Maker Communications
Interest-Creating Opening
Questions
Recommendation
Commitment
Setting Up the Next Action

Questioning is the foundation for professional sales. People will buy for their reasons, not yours.

However, most conventional wisdom on questioning in sales deals with using open probes versus closed questions. Old-school literature and trainers assert, "Never ask a question someone can answer with a 'no'." That statement is bunk, intimates that you should be manipulative, and focuses solely on the mechanics of questioning. The **quantity** of information isn't nearly as important as the quality of information.

You need to ask questions that uncover information you can use to help the person buy. If you simply have a collection of facts that aren't working in your favor, your call screeches to a halt at a dead-end.

There are four categories in which you need to gather information on professional sales and prospecting calls.

1. Facts

Just like the classic old TV cop show, Dragnet, you need the facts about the person's situation. However, most salespeople spend all of their time here. "How large is your operation?", "How many people?", "What do you buy now?", and so on. We certainly need facts, but factual questions bore the answerer, since they see no benefit to them in answering. With factual questions, eventually you reach the point where the prospect thinks, "When is this going to be over?" Get the facts, then move on. Better yet, get as much of this info as you can before even getting to the decision maker.

2. Problems

As quickly as possible, you need to uncover the "pain" or problem that is troubling the person or organization.

People will only take action if they perceive there is some problem they'd like to solve, or if they could enhance their present situation in some way. You need to determine how they view their circumstances. Sometimes they readily state their problem, or better yet, they call you with it. Other times, you need to query them to determine if there is a perceived problem at all, and if not, if it's worth your while to determine if you could develop a need with questions.

3. Costs of the Problem

OK, you know they have pain. Here you want to magnify it. As terrible as it sounds, you want to make them feel badly about their problem. Open their eyes to realize it's worse than they thought. Most salespeople do not expound enough in this area. By getting the prospect to agree that not only they have a problem, but that it's having immense negative implications, they will essentially justify the price of what you're selling. Here are some questioning ideas:

> *"Can you measure in dollars what that's costing you?"*
> *"What effect is that having on your business?"*
> *"How has that hindered you?"*

4. Benefits of Solving the Problem

Now that you've made them feel like topsoil, it's time to build them up with questions. You'll prompt them to tell you what they would gain by erasing their problem. Just as with the previous category, the more specific the better.

> *"What would that be worth to you in terms of increased sales?"*
> *"Exactly how much do you think you'd save?"*

Use the Iceberg Theory of Questioning To Get The Best Information

When you see an iceberg glistening in the water, what do you really see?

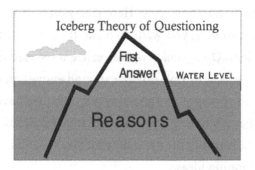

Only a small portion of the iceberg. You see just the tip. The bulk of it is below the water level. (I'm getting to a sales point here, trust me).

When you ask a question, the first answer you hear is the tip of the iceberg. Everything below the water level is the good stuff . . . the information you really can use: the reason behind the initial answer.

Problem is, many salespeople quit after they have the "tip" information, when the "below the water level" information will tell them, why, precisely, the prospect/customer says what they do.

And **that's** the information we need to help them buy.

For example, let's say a sales rep for a human resources prospective-employee testing service receives a business reply card or an Internet lead requesting information. The sales rep, after introducing himself, asks the question,

"Why are you looking to do employee testing?"

The prospect responds, *"We feel that we need to do a better job screening our applicants so we don't make hiring mistakes."*

The sales rep, who has been selling this service for several years and feels he has 'been there and done that' thinks he has a grasp on the situation and begins a presentation on the testing service. The prospect says, "OK, that sounds interesting. Send me out whatever information you have and we'll give it some consideration."

The sales rep complies. He schedules a follow-up for seven days later. Keeps getting voice mail on repeated attempts, with no return calls from the prospect.

The cycle continues.

Oh, by the way, this experienced sales rep has a problem with lots of prospects in his pipeline, but complains about prospects not buying, and how he can't reach them.

The Skilled Sales Rep

Let's look at another sales rep who knows how to "lower the water level" and learn more of the reason behind what people say.

Prospect: "We feel that we need to do a better job screening our applicants so we don't make hiring mistakes."

Sales Rep: "Tell me more."

Prospect: "Well, we've hired a few people over the past year that just didn't work out. They seemed good in the initial interviews, but apparently we were missing something."

Sales Rep: "What do you mean?"

Prospect: "They were able to talk a good game, but when it came time to actually do the work, they lacked what it took."

Sales Rep: "That's not uncommon. What does it take to do well?"

Prospect: "For our customer service positions, we need people who can handle repetitive tasks all day long without becoming bored, remain calm under pressure from irate callers, and be able to think quickly on their feet to resolve problems that involve some math calculations."

Sales Rep: "I believe we can help you with that. Tell me a bit more about your past experiences. About how many people have you hired that didn't work out?"

Prospect: "Almost embarrassed to say . . . probably 10 out of 20."

Sales Rep: "Wow. Any idea of what it costs to hire and train someone for that position."

Prospect: "I hate to even think about it. After newspaper advertising, our interviewing, and two weeks of product training, and their wages, it's got to be a few thousand dollars per person."

Lower the Water Level

To lower the water level, your goal is to keep them talking about their needs, desires and concerns. You want the real reasons behind their initial answers.

The first important step is discipline. Resist the tendency to jump in and present. Instead, question more. Use instructional statements such as,

> *"Tell me more."*
> *"Please go on."*
> *"Elaborate on that for me please."*
> *"I'd like to know more about that."*
> *"Please continue."*

And when they touch on a need, embellish it. Quantify it. Have them discuss the implications of it. You'll undoubtedly find yourself selling more as a result.

Quality Questions Get Quality Answers

Keep in mind that how you phrase a question can make a huge difference in the answer you get. Plus it can affect the attitude of the responder.

For example, I remember when my daughter was in high school, and I caught myself before saying this to her: *"Do you want to have to stay home all weekend because you still haven't cleaned your room?"* Well, duh. What did I expect her to say?

Of course, upon examining my objective, it was to get her to clean her room, and not alienate her in the process. So I rephrased it before opening my mouth:

"I want to make sure you're able to do what you want this weekend. When will your room be totally clean so I can inspect it?"

Yes, the quality of your question dictates the quality of your answer. Let's look at more examples:

Examples

Question: *"Are you a decision maker on this?"*
Better Question: *"Will anyone else, beside yourself, be taking a look at this before you decide to do it?"*

Question: *"It's the final offer, take it or leave it. What do you want to do?"*
Better Question: *"I recommend you take advantage of it, since it's going to be the best offer we have available. Would you like to move on it?"*

Question: *"Why?"*
Better Question: *"What was the reasoning behind that decision?"*

So how do you get better at questioning?

Some people seem to just have that knack for being tactful and "smooth." Other people are painfully blunt and awkward. The desired result comes from analyzing questions you use now, and the answers. Ask yourself, what could I have said to get a better response?

The key to being smooth and effective with questioning is work.

It means determining what you want someone thinking as a result of your call, and then working backward from that result, thinking of the appropriate questions, and then brainstorming for their answers.

And then repeating the process. Almost like planning chess moves in advance.

And then, internalizing where you'll go with every possible answer. That my friend, is work, but it's also how you succeed.

How About Some "How?" Questions?

A while ago I saw a TV commercial for Ping, the golf club company. The theme of the commercial was how Ping built its fine reputation by always asking, "How?"

> *HOW could they make a better putter?*
> *HOW could they make golf more enjoyable with their equipment?*

That's when I dragged my rear out of the chair, grabbed a pen and started scribbling lots of ways that we as salespeople can use "how" with our prospects and customers.

A few points on these questions:

• I've grouped these questions into categories, but you'll see that many of them are interchangeable.

• They're not in a particular order, although some could be used as good follow-up questions in response to their answers to a previous question.

• Also keep in mind that you wouldn't necessarily use just "how" questions exclusively. Mix in the Who, What, Where, and Why questions.

• I have Commitment and Closing, and Objections questions here, even though we could have put them in those chapters.

• As you read them, think about how you can use and/or adapt these for your own calls. Better yet, take notes.

FACT-GATHERING AND QUALIFYING QUESTIONS

"How do you get new business?"
"How could you get more?"
"How could we help you get more?"
"How do you plan on achieving your sales goals this year?"
"How does the purchasing process work at your business?"
"How are decisions like these typically made?"
"How is money normally budgeted?"

"How did you make the decision last time?"
"How could you use our product/service?"
"How did you select the previous vendor?"
"How do you evaluate new vendors?"

NEED IDENTIFICATION/DEVELOPMENT AND PAIN-ENHANCING QUESTIONS

"How did that work last time?"
"How often does that happen?"
"How does that affect other departments?"
"How are you doing it now?"
"How is your situation unique?"
"How could it be done better?"
"How can we help you do it better?"
"How do you see this developing?"
"How could it be improved?"
"How would you describe your present level of service/ satisfaction?"
"How are you going to fix the situation?"
"How did you handle it last time?"
"How does that problem impact other departments?"
"How long has it been going on?"
"How much does it cost you?"
"How much time does it take now?"
"How is it being handled now?"
"How will you handle it?"
"How did you/your employees/your customers react?"

"How does that make them feel?"

"How does that make you feel?"

"How did that happen?"

"How will you prevent it from happening again?"

"How would you define good service?"

"How would you describe...?"

"How does poor quality affect the final product?"

"How much do you think you would save if that problem was solved?"

"How would you use it if you had it?"

CLOSING/COMMITMENT QUESTIONS

"How can we make this work?"

"How can we make this happen?"

"How about starting out with a trial order?"

"How can we get approval?"

"How would you like to proceed?"

"How soon can we get started?"

"How about starting now?"

"How many do you want to start with?"

"How do you see us proceeding?"

"How fast will you need this?"

"How much will you need to start off with?"

"How can we be the ones that you'll choose?"

"How can we be part of the bidding process?"

"How do you want to pay for this?"

"How do you want this delivered?"

ADDRESSING RESISTANCE AND OBJECTIONS

"How much is 'too much'?"
"How could we solve that?"
"How much resistance do you expect internally?"
"How can we both make this work?"
"How much of an issue is that, really?"
"How do we get around this issue?"
"How can you/we find the money?"

CUSTOMER SERVICE

"How can I help?"
"How can I be of service?"
"How could we improve?"
"How are we doing?"
"How can we change?"
"How can we do it better?"
"How can I fix it so you're satisfied?"
"How have we done for you?"

QUESTIONS TO ASK YOURSELF

"How can I change?"
"How could I increase my sales and production by 30% this quarter?"
"How am I going to reach my goals?"
"How should I start?"

How Many Questions Should You Ask at a Time?

At a social function I was talking to a guy who asked five questions in a row, didn't listen to any of the answers, and only used his questions as a springboard to talk about himself.

Since I didn't take much interest in what he was pitching (he shoved his business card into my hand) I watched and listened as he did that with several other people he met.

Sure, we all know we should ask questions. But the effort is wasted if they're not asked in the right way, or you don't listen to the answers.

KEY SALES POINT

When a listener hears a question, their mind immediately is conditioned to begin searching for answers. However, when several questions are posed in rapid-fire sequence, you leave the person confused as to which one they should answer first. And, some questions are not answered at all if you don't give them an opportunity.

For example, read this scenario without stopping to think about each question, as if you were the person hearing the questions:

Caller: *"And what do you feel your company needs most regarding boosting morale and enthusiasm? Do you think it would be*

> *compensation related ... or maybe training? And how does that*
> *affect performance in all of the departments?"*

Did you feel like a spinning top, rotating around trying to focus on the questions coming from all directions? Same thing happens with prospects and customers.

Effective Questioning Guidelines

1. **Ask one question at a time.** If it's not important enough to stand on its own, don't ask it.

2. **After you ask it, shut up.** If they don't answer immediately, resist the urge to answer it for them or follow up with another one. They're likely thinking about what they're going to say.

3. **After they apparently have finished, remain quiet for 1-2 more seconds.** You might get additional information, and it ensures you don't interrupt.

4. **Follow-up their answer with a related question.** Don't ping-pong around from subject to subject. For example, if they answered with, "I believe the main problem we have right now is a lack of motivation," a logical next query would be, "Oh, what are some specific situations where you've seen a lack of motivation?"

5. **Be confident in your questioning.** One reason people ask multiple questions is that they aren't comfortable asking questions. The only way you're going to truly help someone is by finding out about them. You're not intruding. You're assisting.

Fielding multiple questions is confusing for the listener, and counter-productive for you. Ask one at a time, and listen!

Summary

You might be wondering how much questioning to do. Well, it depends on what you are looking to accomplish on your call. If you are simply looking to set an appointment for a face-to-face meeting, I suggest enough questioning to gather some basic information and pique their curiosity. Then your recommendation will be for the meeting so you both can continue the process.

On the more complex end, your questioning can go much deeper. In my case where I am proposing an entire training program development, delivery and follow-up that can reach six figures, I've had calls run an hour long, primarily with questions.

You'll likely be somewhere in between. What I have found, however, is that most salespeople don't question enough. That results in recommendations that are not on-target as well as they could be.

Keep this in mind—and feel free to Tweet it out (@ArtSobczak):

People buy because of their "why." You need to find that out.

YOUR ACTION STEPS

Write out initial questions you will ask your prospect/customer. Then anticipate possible answers, and then plan your next questions.

6 Your Sales Recommendation

CALL PROCESS

Pre-Call Planning
Pre-Decision Maker Communications
Interest-Creating Opening
Questions
Recommendation
Commitment
Setting Up the Next Action

After your questioning you are now ready to move to the next phase: your recommendation for the next step, which includes the description of the results of taking that action. It is here where you at last talk about your product/service. But again, you must include the RESULT, not just the product/service itself.

I could sum up this chapter with just a few words, but that would leave a lot of blank space. So I'll expand on this basic concept:

Present only what people are interested in, based upon what they told you in your questioning.

Some sales training spends inordinate amounts of time on sales presentations. Not mine. In fact I don't even like to call it "presentation" since that implies more of a one-way monologue. I tell people I want them to talk less about their products or services. It's called "objection prevention."

Just like the entire call is a process, so too is the Recommendation a process.

When you've reached that magic moment when you feel it is finally time, here are your steps:

1. **Transition From Your Questioning.** Let them know you're done questioning, and spark interest—again—in having them listen to you:

   "Luke, based on what you told me about the existing insurance coverage on your business, and the added liability exposure you have, I believe I have something here that will cover you completely, at about the same premium you're paying now."

2. **Paraphrase Your Understanding.** Right out of Sales 101, rephrase in your eloquently persuasive—and slightly embellished—way, the needs, concerns, desires, and values they just related to you:

> *"Let's just review what we've discussed so far to make sure I understand it completely. Botom line, you feel you've been neglected by your present agent, except when it came time to renew your policy. And, you feel he's charging you an outrageous premium for the amount of coverage you now need since you're manufacturing toxic chemicals. Is that right?"*

I love this phase so much. Execute it well, and they have just written your recommendation for you. Think about it. If you ask that question at the end and they concur, they have just agreed with what they need.

3. **Present the results of what you can deliver.** Only talk about what they told you they're interested in. Period.

> *"Luke, by switching to my agency you would get the attention you deserve, and pay a reasonable premium for more than enough coverage. First, we would (present proof of each claim you made)..."*

4. **Get Commitment.** You're involved in a conversation at this point, either answering questions, or listening to buying signals. If the questions are buying or possession signals such as "That

sounds good," or, "Do we pay the premium to your agency or to the corporate headquarters?", ask for commitment.

> *"Should we get started?"*
>
> *"You can pay it directly to us. Should we prepare the paperwork?"*

Make your recommendations conclusive.

Leave no doubt as to what they should do.

You're the expert here. Don't just wish they'll come to the conclusion you'd like, and hope they volunteer to take action on their own. I've heard reps leave things up in the air with a weak phrase like, *"So keep us in mind when you feel you'd like to make a switch."* Most people avoid tough decisions.

State your suggestion explicitly so all they have to do is react to it—even if that means resisting it.

> *"Pat, based on everything we've discussed, you'd show a savings from day one on the program. I recommend I overnight the paperwork to you so you can OK it and have it back by Monday. Would you like to do that?"*

It's quite simple. Make a presentation before you know what someone wants, and you're selling. Make it after, and you help them buy. What would you rather do?

Recommendation Tips

People buy results. I can't emphasize enough how much I like the word "results" in place of benefits. It's much more descriptive of what people really want. They don't care diddly about the product or service itself, they get excited about the end result—the picture or feeling—they enjoy from owning or using it. Forget about your product or service, and concentrate on the results you deliver.

Prepare sensory descriptions of your results. Think about how your results are seen, felt physically and emotionally, tasted, and heard. Remember, you want to help them experience, in advance, the results they can enjoy.

> *"And just think how much easier it will be for you to prepare training. Instead of spending hours after work doing the research you said you hate, you can simply flip to the appropriate topic in your Leader's Guide for that month, circle the questions you'd like to use, and listen and moderate while your reps learn through their own discussion."*

Preface results with a reminder. When presenting several results as part of your overall sales message, precede each with a reminder of the pain they want to avoid or eliminate, or the pleasure they desire.

For example,

> *"And here's what will help you avoid those lawsuits you were worried about..."*
> Or, *"And here's where you'll save big money..."*

Use specific numbers. If you present round numbers like 50%, or $100, they tend to be questioned more, or negotiated against more enthusiastically than specific numbers, such as 52%, or $104. People believe more thought and research went into arriving at precise numbers, whereas rounded numbers seem to be pulled out of the air.

Present just a few benefits. Instead of presenting all of your "benefits," present only a few, but in several different ways. After identifying their hot button, use various terms to describe the feelings they'll have by buying from you.

The psychology here is that you are more likely to believe something if it agrees with thoughts already existing in your consciousness. And it's not always necessary that you've totally accepted the idea . . . just that you haven't disagreed with it.

It's like saying, "Yeah, I've heard that before. It must have merit." Then the more it's repeated, the more firmly embedded it becomes.

Create Urgency in Your Sales Message

Often prospects may be interested in what you have, but they see no hurry in buying. The postponement stall is very common. Here are some ideas which may apply to your sales recommendation to help hasten the decision:

> *"... the price will go up on a certain date/a limited time offer."*
> *"... there is a chance the price will go up (if dictated by unpredictable conditions)."*
> *"... production time will take (x) length of time."*
> *"... delivery will take (x) length of time."*
> *"... an order now ensures availability."*
> *"... every day of delay means lost savings."*
> *"... every day of delay means lost income/convenience."*

People will only take action on a need or pain or problem if they see it as urgent enough to do so now. Creating urgency is not being pushy. It is a way of helping the prospect make a quicker decision, which will be to their advantage.

Define your experience. What does "experience" mean to you? It is a word that might mean nothing to your listeners. If you feel they are interested in your track record, give examples of results. Instead of, "We have experience in that area," tell them,

> *"We have worked with four companies in that industry and helped every one beat production quotas."*

"I have a list of satisfied customers who have used it."
"For six years companies have been coming back to us, and referring us to others."

Your "Benefits" Might Not Be

It's good to listen to your recordings and examine some of the routine phrases you use to explain your company and capabilities. Some of these might be uninspiring—or worse, resistance inducing—yet you're using them consistently. Examples to watch out for:

"We've been in business for over _____ years." Or,
"We're the largest."
And that helps me . . . how?

"We're the most experienced in the industry."
According to what criteria, and how does that affect me?

"We're a national company with 30 locations."
What if I'm a little company doing business in my local hamlet?

"We have a commitment to quality."
That's nice. Who doesn't? How will that help me, specifically?

"We were the first to ..."
So? What have you done since then, and how will it help me?

"We provide cost-effective solutions ..."
Uh-huh, and that means ... what ... exactly, as it relates to what I want?

Always Have Something Meaningful to Say

Here are a couple of ideas to keep in mind in order to ensure your pronouncements actually mean something.

1. Use **"which means,"** and **"what this will do for you is..."** to ensure you're describing results.

2. Get information about the prospect/customer and their concerns, desires, and dilemmas before spouting off about what you can do.

It really is that simple, IF you did your work in the questioning part of the call.

Again, only talk about what you can do after you have asked questions. Otherwise, you are talking about what you **think** they should buy, instead of what they want. And that creates objections.

Be Sure Your Examples Are All About THEM

A sales rep cold-called me the other day and was reading a pitch for website search engine optimization. Aside from numerous other mistakes he made (not knowing anything about me or my company, reading from a script, having a horrible opening, not asking questions . . .) he repeatedly said, ". . . and I feel that . . .", " . . . and I know that you will . . ."

What's a justifiable feeling in response to that "I" language?

> *"Who cares what YOU think? You don't know me, or anything about me."*

I can't say this often enough: The not-so-secret, secret to sales success is determining and understanding what someone wants, and then showing them how they can get it, or giving it to them.

And that means gathering information before the call, and during the call. Then, when it's time to make your recommendation, you know it's on target. It has to be, because if you did your job, they told you what they're interested in.

And when you're presenting, use a "YOU" language, not "I." Further, use plenty of personalized and customized examples.

Examples sell. Anyone can make a statement, and most sales-people do. But, when it's backed up by proof . . . examples . . . then it carries credibility. Plus it adds visualization to the sales process by phone.

For example, it will be easy for you to see which statement has more impact.

> *"Our service will cut down on processing time."*

> *"Our service will cut down on the time you said it takes for you to enter orders, print shipping forms and labels, and get the order out the door faster to meet the requirements you mentioned. I have customers in your industry who have doubled the number of orders they're able to handle in a day."*

Take every statement you use to describe the benefits/results you deliver. Brainstorm for the sensory terms and descriptions that bring those results to life. Then find several concrete examples of how others have already experienced those results. Commit them to memory so they're always a part of your presentations.

Make Your Recommendations Come to Life

I always snicker when someone says, "The phone can't be used as a serious sales tool. Buyers need to see someone face-to-face."

They might as well say, "I'm not very good on the phone at describing what we can do for customers."

It's also like when people say, "We sell a service. You can't sell that by phone."

Listen carefully, my friend: people don't buy products or services. They buy the end result. They buy a picture of the end result—with them in the picture. Regardless of whether you're selling a product or service, you're selling the same thing: the result.

People buy because they experience (see, feel, hear, taste, or touch) in advance, the results of using/owning/feeling the results of your products or services. Describe those results in sensory terms and you'll sell more.

And the more you can get them involved over the phone, the better.

Ask them to write something down when you make a point.

Ask them to punch numbers into their calculator.

If you sent literature, or if you know they have your catalog, ask them to grab it. Then have them turn to a page with you, and discuss what you both see. Do the same with your website. This helps to bridge the visual gap.

Also, emotionally, you can use words to help them "see" what you're talking about. Use graphic descriptions, with colors, action, taste, or smell to stimulate their senses.

For example, if someone said, *"This cleaner will really do the job for you,"* that's not too moving.

But, consider the difference if someone said,

> *"This cleaner will wipe away stains as easy as a wet towel erases a whiteboard. And it doesn't have that sterile, hospital smell. It leaves a pleasant scent, kind of like a bowl of fresh fruit."*

Great salespeople have no problem using the phone to describe the results they deliver. That's because they understand those results, and how they fit with what the prospect/customer wants.

Make that visual and sensory image easy for them. One way to do this is to refer to objects in the person's environment, or to relate to images that are familiar to the listener.

For example,

> *"If you take a look at your computer keyboard, it's about that same size."*
> *"It's very lightweight ... about the same as your standard office stapler."*
> *"The unit would easily fit on the corner of a desktop, without hindering the ability to spread your work all over the top of the desk."*
> *"The texture is comparable to regular commercial grade office carpet."*

> *"If you took your hands and held them about twelve inches apart, that's how wide it is."*
> *"I'd say the color is the same as a manila file folder."*
> *"Take a look at the top of your desk. It's about that tall from the floor."*

The more senses you can engage, the better. Get your listener actively involved, and you enhance your chances with them.

Don't Present Your Way OUT Of the Sale

And finally, let's end with some advice about knowing when to quit recommending.

A sales rep for a subscription publication called and said,

> *"The reason I'm calling is that your subscription runs out this month, and I was calling to see if you wanted to keep that going ... or what you wanted to do ... (nervous pause) or if you just wanted to let it run out?"*

Even though I had not given any thought to my plans regarding the subscription, his invitation finalized my decision. He made it so easy to agree, "Yeah, just go ahead and let it run out."

On the other hand, the law of inertia was in his favor if he would have chosen to stop talking after making his positive suggestion.

There are several points here that are elementary, but carry so much impact. And they're violated regularly.

- Don't talk yourself out of a sale.
- Shut up.
- Don't make negative recommendations.
- Make positive recommendations and then pause. Regardless of how awkward the silence might feel.

Here's another example:

After getting the question, "What is your best price?" I heard a sales rep say, *"Well, it's $799."*

No reaction from the prospect.

"... but we could probably give you a $150 new customer discount."

No reaction from the prospect.

"And I probably can get another $80 knocked off."

"OK, that sounds good," said the prospect, who probably would have bought had the rep simply stated the first price and clammed up.

Get comfortable with silence. Don't feel a compelling urge to keep talking. When you're with someone in person, keep in mind what they're doing during the silent times . . . thinking, stroking their chin, pondering your offer . . . they are doing the same on the phone.

YOUR ACTION STEPS

What will you commit to DO as a result of this chapter?

7 Getting Commitment

CALL PROCESS

Pre-Call Planning
Pre-Decision Maker Communications
Interest-Creating Opening
Questions
Recommendation
Commitment
Setting Up the Next Action

When clients tell me their reps need work on "closing techniques," I begin worrying, since it's typically indicative of a larger problem: not moving the call and the sales process to the point where the "close" is appropriate.

We should minimize or eliminate the word "close" and replace it with "commitment."

"Closing" implies an end; what you really want instead is to open and build a relationship. And to do that, you need constant movement on each of your calls towards an objective. This movement happens when your prospects/customers commit to doing something between now and the next call.

The Commitment Phase Validates What Has Happened So Far

A football team doesn't throw the long bomb every time it gets the ball at its own 20-yard line. A man doesn't ask a woman to marry him after one date. Neither tactic is a high percentage play. And just like on sales calls, to achieve the objective, you need to move forward, enjoying little successes along the way. The momentum is then behind you, and the ultimate commitment is much easier, since you've traveled closer to the objective. Therefore, the "close" shouldn't be the major part of the call; it's the validation of what's been covered so far.

Attitude is More Important Than Technique

Scan the sales section in bookstores or libraries or search "Sales closing" on amazon and you'll find lots of nonsense on "closing techniques." Many contain the tired old phrases that cause people to bristle, like the guy from the Better Business Bureau the other day who, after his three-minute pitch about how I "qualified for membership" (by virtue of having a business, I guess) would like to drop by at *3:30 on Wednesday, or 9:00 on*

Thursday. Which would be better for you?" Neither, I told him, since that would imply I saw some value in meeting with him, which he hadn't shown me yet. He threw the long bomb too early, before moving the relationship forward, and tried to rely on a technique.

I say forget about technique, at least initially. Work on your attitude. Get out of your comfort zone, ask more, ask larger, and you'll sell more. It's this simple: have an asking attitude and you'll do it. Be shy about asking, and you'll miss out. Maybe even lose your job. Don't let that happen.

Commitment Questions You Can Use

Here are ideas for commitment questions you can use or adapt to move the relationship forward.

> *"What will happen between now and our next contact?"*
> *"If you like what you see in the sample, will you buy?"*
> *"Are you comfortable taking this to the boss with your recommendation that you go with it?"*
> *"So you will have those inventory figures prepared by the next time we speak, is that right?"*
> *"You're going to survey your staff and get their input on what features they'd like to see, and you'll have the information by our next call, correct?"*
> *"By when will you have had a chance to go through the material so we can speak again?"*

"Is this the program that you'd personally like to invest in?"

"If you do decide to change vendors before my next call, will you call me?"

"The next time you need supplies, would you buy them from me?"

"When you send out your Request for Proposals, may I be included?"

"Shall we get started?"

"Would you like to buy it?"

"Why don't I ship you one?"

"May I sign you up?"

"If the proposal contains all of these items, will you approve it and go with our plan?"

"Can we finalize the paperwork?"

Listen for "Future Tense" Statements as Buying Signals

Of course knowing when to ask for commitment enhances your chances for success. Be aware of signs that they are agreeing with you.

A strong buying signal to watch out for: when they speak in the present or future tense regarding your product or service, or the other details that would be affected by a purchase. This means that emotionally they already have bought. They see themselves in the picture, already using your product or service.

For example,

> *"I guess we'd make room in the back office for the unit."*
> *"Hmm, I'm not sure how many people I would train on that installation."*
> *"We will probably need to adjust our production schedule to meet the new demand."*

Think of what statements you hear that indicate emotional ownership and be on the lookout for them. Upon hearing them, move toward the solid commitment.

Closing Questions

Here are some additional commitment and closing questions.

> *"Where do we stand right now?"*
> *"What is the next step?"*
> *"How shall we proceed?"*
> *"Is there anything else we need to cover before moving forward?"*
> *"Have we covered everything, or are we ready to get going?"*
> *"I suggest we wrap up the details, OK?"*

It's All About HOW You Say It

There's a difference between simply saying the words, and REALLY SAYING THE WORDS! This is particularly true when it comes to asking for commitment and closing the sale.

In observing sales calls recently, it was astounding the difference that tone of voice made when asking for the business. The reps who used a tentative, sheepish tone didn't inspire much confidence in the listeners. Therefore their successes were minimal.

On the other hand, when sales reps projected an air of matter-of-factness in their voices (which wasn't pushy or arrogant), prospects seemed to naturally comply with the reps' requests.

To further illustrate this point, put yourself in the position of buyer. How would you feel if a salesperson submissively mumbled, "Well, do you think you might want to do this?"

Now imagine the authoritative voice of someone who knew in their heart that this was the best choice for you:

"Let's go ahead and get you started, OK?"

Listen to recordings of your calls. Pay careful attention to not only what you say, but the way you're saying it. Ask yourself, Would I be inspired by that voice? If not, work to change your tone, because that's what adds the impact.

Get Commitments on Every Call

Never agree to place a follow-up call until you've gotten commitment they'll do something between now and the next contact. It can be as minor as them agreeing to review your catalog
and selecting items they would like to discuss next time. Of
course, the ultimate commitment is agreeing to buy from you
on this call. You can qualify a prospect by their level of commitment. If they won't do anything, they're likely not interested.
And why would you waste time calling someone like that back?

Focus on moving your relationship forward, get in the asking
habit, get commitments on every call, and you'll "close" more sales.

Wishing for the Business is Not Enough. You Need to ASK

I'll end this chapter with an observation, and a number of tips
and commitment examples.

A struggling sales rep hadn't hit quota in, well, ever.

The manager couldn't figure it out. It was apparent to me after
listening to just a few calls.

See if you can pick out the commonality in all of these examples from calls:

> *"Keep us in mind the next time you need something."*
> *"Let us know if we can help."*
> *"We'd love to work with you on that project."*
> *"Let me know if I can answer any more questions on this price quote."*

These phrases ask for **no** commitment. They're not proactive. They don't ask for the sale—they wish for it.

Every time you or your salespeople end a telephone call (or an inside visit), there should be a request for some type of commitment to ensure they're moving closer to a sale.

Granted, a sale might not take place on every call, but we can likely get some type of commitment each time.

Here are plenty of brief tips you can use to ask for and get more commitments and sales.

• Don't always judge success by the "yes" answers you get. Measure your attempts. Set a goal for the number of times you'll ask for the business today. Celebrate when you reach that goal. The sales naturally follow.

- Closing Question: **"Gene, we seem to be in agreement that these motors are what you're looking for. What do you suggest we do?"**

- Closing Question: **"Kelly, what can we do together to speed up the process and make this happen?"**

- Closing Question: **"Are you thinking about getting three of them?"** Use whatever amount would be just a tad higher than what they likely would do. This prompts a decision, or more conversation.

- Ask for commitment with conviction. Your tone of voice does matter.

- Those who expect more, get more. Don't sell yourself short when asking for the sale. Ask big.

- A question to help them determine what should happen next: **"What is the next step?"**

- Closing Question: **"We could have these delivered by Tuesday. What would you like me to do?"**

- To upsell, don't mention the next price break, as in "You can get a better deal if you buy 50." Instead, simply mention how many more they need to get the price. **"You'll save $1.50 per unit by getting only five more."**

- Help them visualize themselves owning and using your product/service. **"If you had this, how do you feel you'd utilize it?"**

- State the agreement you've reached, then ask for the major commitment: **"Jan, since we're in agreement that this is what you're looking for, and it's within your budget, let's go ahead and get the paperwork started, OK?"**

- Closing question: **"Sounds to me like you've already decided to go with these tools. Am I right?"**

- Closing question: **"Do you have further questions, or are we ready to proceed?"**

- Closing question: **"Is there anything else you need to know to move ahead with this order?"**

- Listen for "possession signals," signs that they've already visualized themselves using your product/service. "What we'd likely do is get enough for each of our locations."

- A major reason customers don't buy more from their vendors: they aren't asked to by the vendor. Be sure you're satisfying every need you possibly can.

- When you're writing up an order, don't say, "Anything else?" We're all conditioned to say "No." Instead, make a tangible recommendation based on what they're already getting, then ask for the sale. For example, "**Many customers who get _____ also find _____ to be of great value because (fill in with the results they realize).**"

- "Pushiness" only occurs when you try to sell someone something they don't want or need. Asking for the sale is not being pushy, assuming you've questioned effectively and made the appropriate recommendation.

- Don't just wish for the sale: "I just wanted to let you know these do come in several colors, and we could even custom order one for you." Be sure there is no question that you are ASKING for it.

- Tie the timing of the next call into their commitment to take some action. "What day do you feel we should speak again, so that you'll have had enough time to collect those specifications?"

Ask for decisions. Don't let people put you off. It wastes your time and money. Equate getting a decision—yes or no—with success. Get in the habit of asking for commitments and sales and you will instantly show increased results.

YOUR ACTION STEPS

Speaking of commitment, what will you commit to DO as a result of this section?

8 Wrap Up and Set Up the Next Action

CALL PROCESS

Pre-Call Planning
Pre-Decision Maker Communications
Interest-Creating Opening
Questions
Recommendation
Commitment
Setting Up the Next Action

Do you ever have problems with follow-up calls, even after you felt the previous call went OK?

Or, how about that gut-knotting feeling of staring at your prospect notes from a previous call as you prepare for the next one, searching for—but not finding—what you'll say on this call that's more inspiring than, *"Well, ahh, I'm just calling you back to see if you got my brochure, and what you think?"*

If you've ever been there—and most of us have—chances are that your previous call didn't end strongly, with a clear summarization of that call, and of what was to happen next, both before the next call, and during it.

Ending a call with, *"OK, I'll just send you out some literature, and give you a call back in a couple of weeks,"* virtually ensures your demise on the next contact.

And rightfully so; there's nothing specific here, no connection between this call and the next, no summarization of the problem, need or interest (if there was any at all), and no confirmation of who's to do what next.

Here's what you should do at the end of your calls to ensure a fluid transition from this contact to the next. (By the way, all of this presumes you didn't get a sale—we're all pretty good at wrapping up those calls.)

How to Wrap Up a Call to Plan the Next

Before ending the call you need to do an overview with your prospect/customer. Summarize,

The Need/Problem, and Their Interest. Revisit what they are interested in, and why.

What They Will Do. At the very minimum you should get commitment they will read your material and prepare questions, test out your sample and evaluate it according to criteria you've both discussed, take your proposal to the committee with their recommendation, and so on. THIS IS CRITICAL! If you don't get a commitment for action, this person might not ever become a customer. Asking for, and getting some type of action commitment is my way of tightly qualifying people. If they're not taking action, why are you calling back?

What You'll Do. Review what you'll do, what you'll send, who you'll speak with, or whatever you promised.

When You'll Talk Next. Don't say, *"How 'bout I call you in a couple of weeks?"* Let them give you a date, and tie it to their commitment:

> *"Carol, by when do you think you will have collected all of the inventory figures we'll need for our next conversation?"*

Not only do you have a date and time, but you have their commitment, again, they'll perform their duties.

The Next-Call Agenda. Go over what's to happen next. It plants a seed as to what they should expect on the following call.

> *"Let me go through what we've covered today. You feel that Advantage Inc. will provide you with better availability, and*

> *you like our customer service policies, and you do want to get*
> *going with that new inventory program we offer, but you need*
> *to wait to get funding in the next budget, which you're going*
> *to suggest, and we'll plan on talking around the first of next*
> *month, when I call you again."*

Get a Graduate Degree in Sales

It's said that we don't learn nearly as much performing an activity as we do after it, by reviewing and analyzing our experience. You can earn a "graduate degree" by simply assessing your calls, committing to take action where improvement is needed, and then beginning preparation for the next contact to the same person. Here's how.

Analyze the Call

Ask, **"What did I like about this call?"** Reinforce a deed well done. What gets rewarded, gets repeated.

Ask, **"What would I have done differently?"** Keep it positive. Don't ask the destructive question, *"What didn't I like?"* And don't darken your attitude with negative self-talk like, *"I really blew that call."* Instead, be positive and action-oriented. By pondering what you could have done differently, you're replaying the call, doing a mental role play, searching for phrases you'll use next time. And that's how you improve.

Prepare Notes, and Plan The Next Call

Review and record what they're doing and what you'll do as a result of this call. Also put in your notes:

Info You Need on the Next Call. Remind yourself what to ask next time.

Possible Next-Call Objectives. What better time to partially plan your next contact, while this one is still fresh in mind.

Opening Statement Ideas. Ditto the previous reason.

What's that you say? Can't take the time after a call to do all this stuff? Think again. These steps actually save you time in preparing your next call, and ensures your calls are as solid as possible.

YOUR ACTION STEPS

What will you commit to DO as a result of this section?

9 The Professional And Successful Way To Deal With Objections

We've completed the call process as I teach it and use it. You might have noticed that I don't have a section in the process itself on objections.

That's because if you follow the process perfectly, we avoid objections.

Ok, I know, they still sometimes occur. That's why we'll cover them now. But I treat objections differently than many sales experts.

How to Deal With Objections

When's the last time someone thanked you for telling them they were flat out wrong? It doesn't happen.

Even though everyone resents being told they're wrong—often getting defensive—most sales training suggests sales reps do exactly that: counter objections and resistance with slick, canned phrases, with insidious names like the "Boomerang Technique," which inherently tells people they're wrong and makes them feel just slightly lower than topsoil.

You'll never change anyone's mind by preaching at them.

For example, think about beliefs you feel strongly about: something political, moral, or even a favorite sports team. If someone simply started refuting everything you believed in, you would likely strengthen your stance, and think of why the other person is wrong.

You can, however, help someone to first *doubt* their beliefs, which is the initial hurdle in opening them up to your ideas.

Get them to *question* their position regarding your offer or ideas.

People believe their ideas more than they do yours.

You can't tell them they're wrong and expect success, but you can help them to doubt their perceptions, which causes them to lower their guard and at least be open to what you have to say. You do this with doubt-creating questions.

Here's how, using some of the principles of the Objection Autopsy explained in a few moments.

1. **Understand the objections you commonly hear.** Write them out. Then list reasons people voice that objection. For example, when they say "Your price is too high," does that mean they can get it cheaper down the street? Or, did they have a predetermined price figure in mind? Or, do they not have enough money in the budget? You'll need to know their rationale (their problem) before you can address the symptom: the objection.

2. **For each of the objection reasons, write out questions that uncover their rationale, and plants seeds of doubt.** For example, for the "price is too high," questions could be,

> *"Are we talking about just the price itself, or the long-term value?"*
> *"What are we being compared to?"*
> *"What price figure did you feel would be appropriate for what you're looking to receive?"*
> *"Take price out of the picture for a moment, do you like this unit better than any other you've seen?"*

Or, take the situation of a wholesale supplier trying to persuade a retailer to carry his product. The retailer says, "We don't need to stock any more lines." The wholesaler could use a canned "objection rebuttal," trotting out market share facts and figures that would prove the retailer wrong—but not change his mind. A doubt-creating approach would use questions:

"How often in the past month have people called and asked for this type of product and you're not able to provide it?", or, *"Have you ever had a situation where someone called and asked about a product like this, but they didn't come in because they found out you didn't have it?"*

Approach objections in a non-adversarial way, and ask questions to root out the reasons. Go through this process, and you'll be better prepared to ask the right questions to plant the seeds of doubt in their mind, opening them up to considering your ideas, therefore softening their resistance.

Preparing for Objections With the Objections Autopsy

When dealing with objections, what we're really doing is backing up and revisiting the questioning part of the call. Because, if the person is resisting your recommendation, it's typically because you either didn't collect enough information to make the best recommendation for what they want, or, they misunderstood what you presented.

Here's the best way I know of to prepare to address objections. It's called the Objection Autopsy, and it helps you think of all possible reasons for the objections you hear, the questions you'll ask upon hearing them, the possible responses . . . and it continues until you have enough information to again make a recommendation that helps the prospect/customer understand why what you have will help them.

1. **Select a common, real objection.** For example, "Your minimum order is too high for me."

2. **Brainstorm all the possible reasons why the objection could be stated.** For any objection, you might have multiple reasons.

3. **Develop opening questions to address the objection** (after isolating it). Isolation question: *"If it weren't for the minimum, would you buy from us?"* If so, *"Let's talk about the minimum then. How much would you say all your orders over a month total, even with your other vendors?"*

4. **Think of their possible answers, and your next responses.**

5. **Continue the process.** This looks like a computer programmer's flow chart. Ultimately you can reach an understanding and agreement together, or you'll determine there's not a fit. And a very important point about objections is that you will not, and can not, answer every one.

Quick Tips For Dealing With Objections

To get them talking after they state an objection, say, **"Tell me more about that."**

The old myth says that "The selling doesn't start until an objection has been expressed." That's garbage. If the sales process had been perfectly executed, an objection wouldn't even occur.

Resistance early in a call is easier to deal with than a major objection later on. Plus it helps you change course when necessary. So, ask for the resistance if it's there. **"What are your thoughts so far?"**

Use the **"Just suppose"** technique. **"Just suppose the money was in the budget. Would you go with it then?"**

Never tell someone they're wrong (even if they are!). Instead, take the responsibility. **"I don't think I explained myself clearly. Here is what I meant when I said ..."**

Handling The "Not Now" Objection

Here's a step-by-step way to address the objection, "The time just isn't right, right now."

As with any objection, you need to break it down gradually with a series of questions. What you don't want to say at this point is, "Oh, OK, when can I call you back." A date is of little use if they're not interested. Because they've then just given you the next date when they'll brush you off again.

Your first move needs to be,

> *"I see. Let's talk about that. First, do you agree that the system/ product/service is something that you would see yourself using?"*

This is critical. It confirms that they're not just blowing you off. No use wasting a series of frustrating follow-up calls to hear the same—or a more creative—objection again. Hey, if you're going to get a definite "I'm not a prospect," get it now.

Now, learning a time frame would be more useful.

> *"When would you see yourself using/getting involved/joining/ buying?"*

Notice the wording here. Speak in terms of their action, what they will do—buy from you. If you just said, *"When can I call you back?"* you're simply asking them for permission to call again, and that's not as desirable as the alternative.

After confirmation of interest, then find out about the delay.

> *"What changes do you anticipate that would make another time right for you?"*

> Or, *"What will make (date) a better time for you?"*
> Or, *"What's going to happen between now and then that will make it a better time?"*

This not only helps to further qualify their intentions (a fuzzy answer here might mean they aren't that hot of a prospect), but it gives you ammo to work with in case they're mistaken about what you've presented, they don't have all the facts yet, or if they aren't convinced about the value and urgency of acting now.

Then, listen very carefully to the answers. Here are possible responses from them, and routes you could take.

They say, "We'll have more money available then."

You could revisit the reasons they're interested. Ask questions to help them tell you what the missed opportunity would be by waiting. Get them to quantify it. For example,

> *"What would you say that is costing you now?"*

Or, if the situation isn't fixed,

> *"How much extra expense will you incur?"*

Let's say you've concluded that they do have a valid reason for waiting, and they agree that they want to work with you. Firm it up at this point. Get commitments.

"OK, if anything changes between now and our next scheduled conversation, will you please call me?"

Or, "Great, so I'm assuming that the next time we speak we can discuss details of implementing the program?"

Notice how you're pre-closing the sale.

After finishing the call, confirm your understanding with a letter or email detailing the points.

Then and there, schedule reminders to keep your name in front of them: postcards, hand-written notes, even after-hours voice mail messages with tidbits of interest to them.

Help Them See Savings

Let's say you've reached the point where you've pointed out the savings you could show for the customer, but they don't see the amount as significant enough to take action over. Your tendency is likely to beat your head against the desk and say, "Dummy, open your eyes." Don't. Instead, analyze the real problem: he simply isn't associating the dollar amount he's overpaying now as a big enough problem, or viewing the savings as a large enough solution to a problem. Therefore, your job is to present it in a way that helps him to think differently.

As with any objection, the first action is to determine if that truly is the only factor keeping them from buying.

Ask,

> *"Is it that your feelings about the savings not being significant enough the only thing keeping you from moving forward?"*

After getting confirmation, then move to the next step.

Consider,

- Putting the savings in terms of profits.

  > *"That's money that drops directly to your bottom line."*

- Profits, in terms of additional sales they would need to get.

  > *"Let's look at this in terms of what you'd need to sell to realize this much profit. Based on your 10% margin, you'd have to sell another $10,000 worth of your products just to show the $1000 profit I'm basically giving you."*

- Relating it to common expenses.

  > *"With these savings you could make the monthly payments on three of your delivery vans. It would be like we're actually buying your trucks!"*

Responses to the "Happy With Present Supplier," Objection

In my **Smart Calling Tips** email newsletter we dealt with the objection/stall, "I'm happy with my present supplier." Here are a few suggestions.

Ask if You Can Quote Anyway

When met with the present supplier satisfaction objection I will often ask if I can quote our comparative product just to make sure they are getting the most value for their money. Very rarely will they refuse a quote. If I have listened well to their application I can highlight how our products meet with their current needs. I will follow up on the quote in a day or two and again highlight the benefits to them. More often than not I have received their next order. *Rick Kendall, Branom Instrument Co*

Ask if You Can Stay in Touch

"That's fine Mr. Client. As you know, there are new products and services that come along every day that are bigger, better, faster and cheaper etc. which is what often separates the successful companies from the unsuccessful ones. In the event that something changes with your current service/supplier would it be alright if I stay in touch? Terrific ... by the way ... is there any particular product or service that you might have an interest in?"

Ask About a Specific Product

In my industry, there tends to be a lot of shortages, especially in the newest of the products. I like to find something that the prospect uses, that I know is hard to find, say a hot new video card, for example, and then ask if he ever has problems getting that item. When he says yes, I mention that if nothing else I would love to be his second source. After all who wants to rely on one source for their products during an allocations period. I like to always start off with the Second Source method because it sounds like you aren't trying to break-up their current relationships with other vendors. *Michael Bechtel, D&H Distributing*

Find the Unhappiness

When someone tells me they are "happy with their present set-up" I respect that answer and simply follow up with, "How often or when will you next evaluate the present set-up?" Depending on that answer I will follow up with, "Under what circumstances would they consider switching their present set-up?" (Which I believe was in your books.) If they open up, and questioning can continue, I do so. However, I can usually at least get those two questions answered which helps in knowing when I should call back again. I deal primarily with CFO's so I want to be respectful of their answer of being "happy with their present set-up". I have found that my time is better spent finding the CFO's that are unhappy with their present set-up and waiting to be approached, rather than trying to make a sincerely happy person switch to my company. I find that there are just as many prospects that are "unhappy" with their set-up as there are that are "happy" with their present set-up. I'll get the "happy" ones down the road when they become "unhappy". Eventually it seems, almost everyone becomes "unhappy" because they are taken for granted by their vendor who becomes too comfortable and lets service slide. Taking the customer for granted will always open the door to competition. I keep in touch so I know when that door begins to open. *Jared Olson, General Service Bureau Inc.*

"Keep Us in Mind" Is Worthless, and What to Do Instead

Let's look at the situations where you don't get the sale or accomplish your objective. There is a right way to handle these that can keep your chances alive for the future.

For example, a sales rep travels nowhere on a prospecting phone call. Because he thinks he's doing something productive, or he's in a rush to minimize the pain and get off the phone, he utters one of these laughable phrases,

> *"Well, keep us in mind, OK?"*
> *"Here's my number, write it down just in case."*
> *"How about I give you a call in six months or so?"*

When I'm the prospect, I really do feel quite guilty—OK, maybe only slightly . . . all right, not the least bit of remorse—when I respond with an "OK, I will keep you in mind." Or when I'm feigning interest and scribbling down their phone number while I'm actually doodling abstract farm animals.

These phrases make liars out of prospects.

Face it. They have no intention of "keeping us in mind," let alone writing down our number. These phrases don't accomplish anything positive, and give no reason for the listener to ever want to consider "keeping you in mind" or calling you.

But you can and should salvage something from these calls. Here's what you should do and say instead.

1. Determine if There Ever Would Be Potential

A money- and time-wasting mistake is hanging on to prospects when there's no shred of evidence that the person is a prospect.

Maybe you've experienced it: these "prospects" are recycled through your CRM system. You peruse the notes, get that aching pang in your stomach recalling your last dead-end call. And since there's nothing leading you to believe they're any better of a prospect today . . . you page through to the next prospect, postponing the inevitable. Or you call and experience either rejection or another put-off.

Another error is letting them go when, indeed, there might be some potential.

What to do instead? Find out for sure. Ask,

> *"Ben, under what circumstances would you ever see yourself considering another vendor?"*

Notice the wording here. It's a question that not only asks if they ever would use someone else, but it also asks for the circumstances that would surround it. For example, I've heard prospects respond, *"Well, I suppose if I ever got into an emergency situation where they weren't able to deliver, I'd have to look elsewhere."*

Then you have an opportunity to pick up on that remark and continue questioning.

On the other hand, if they say, *"Look, you're wasting your time buddy. Quit calling me,"* write them off and move on.

And feel good about it, since you obtained a decision. When you contine to recycle contacts who will never buy from you, that's "rescheduling the next brushoff." Your irreplaceable commodity is time. Protect it with all you have, since you'll never get it back.

2. Proactively Give Them Something to Think About

To reiterate, "Keep us is mind," is a worthless phrase. If you truly want someone to keep you in mind, give them a reason. And tie it into a problem they might experience—a problem you could solve. That might prompt them to not only think of you, but better yet, to call you.

Let's say a sales rep knows she can help a company lower their property taxes, but they either don't see the need at this point, or don't believe her. She might end the call with,

> *"I still feel we can help you. Here's something to consider: when you review your property tax itemization, take a look at the specific valuation and charges for your out-of-state properties. If you feel those taxes are high and question them, keep in mind we are specialists on the tax laws in every state, and know the best way to challenge, and eventually lower the bill. I'll send you an email with my contact info in it, so keep it in your tax file, and give me a call then if you feel it would help."*

Don't make liars out of people. The process is simple. Determine if there ever will be potential. If not, move them out of your system and look at that as a victory.

If there is, give them examples of situations to look for, and associate them with the problem you can solve. When they do experience these problems, you'll have a greater chance of them thinking of you.

YOUR ACTION STEPS

What will you commit to DO as a result of this section?

10 Don't Confuse "Reflex Resistance" With Real Objections

Humans are born with only two fears: the fear of falling, and the fear of loud noises. Babies react with a startled reflex to both.

I truly believe there's another one—the fear of being sold. Because, most people react instinctively with a reflex response if they feel a sales pitch coming on.

These are instinctive brush off's:

> *"We don't need any."*
> *"I'm happy with my present service."*
> *"I'm not interested."*
> *"I'm busy right now."*

And you know what? Brush off's usually work!

However, since brush off's are instinctive reflex responses, they are very shallow. There is no real reason behind them, other than the natural human need to protect ourselves from being sold. Here is a very important point I'm going to make regarding brush off's that will help you not fall victim to them:

You can stand up to the brush off by getting the other person to talk.

If you can simply get the other person talking, their mind is off their reflex response, and it's on your question. Let's look at one:

Prospect: "Hello, this is Joan Stevens."

Caller: "Hi Ms. Stevens, I'm Mike Hamilton with Heartland Supply. We specialize in providing low-cost mailroom and packaging supplies. I'd like to discuss your mailroom, and what you use, to determine if what we have would be of any benefit to you.

Prospect: "I'm happy with my present supplier."

Caller: "I see. Who are you using now?

Prospect: "We buy from Packing Plus."

Caller: "Oh sure. What do you get from them."

Prospect: "Well, we buy the standard boxes, padded envelopes, tape, plus a few specialty items."

Caller: "Oh, tell me about those . . . the specialty items."

Prospect: "In our operation, we often send out large orders that require . . ."

Did you notice that there was resistance at the beginning of the call? The person put forth a reflex response that stated, we're happy with our present supplier. Some sales reps would have said, "Oh, OK. Keep us in mind if we can ever help. Bye."

Instead, this caller was curious. He acknowledged the response, and asked more questions, therefore melting the resistance by getting the other person to talk.

Asking a question is effective because it takes the prospect's focus off of the stall, and gets them involved in answering a specific question. Any time you can change the subject from the brush off to a substantive topic, you have essentially ignored the brush off, while gathering useful information in the process.

Other Examples

Here are some other ways to avoid brush off's:

> **Brush Off:** "We're not interested."
> **Caller:** "I don't blame you. Most of my best customers also first said that when I first called them. Tell me, what types of situations do you run into when . . .?"

> **Brush Off:** "We're not in the market for any advertising."
> **Caller:** "I see. I noticed your ads in Business News. What else are you doing to promote your new location?"

It's very difficult to deal with a vague general statement like a reflex response. That's why they work so well for prospects. But, when you get someone talking, you have more information to deal with, which helps you ask more relevant questions, and make points of interest.

After hearing these, you might be asking yourself, "Should we just ignore their reflex responses?"

Yes.

Remember, most people don't even think about what they say when they give the response. It's as natural to them as squinting their eyes when walking into the bright light after coming out of the dark movie theatre. It's a reaction to protect themselves.

By getting them talking, you have taken their mind off of the response.

OK, here is your assignment on dealing with reflex response resistance. Think of the one or two reflex responses that you most commonly hear. Again, these can be "I'm not interested," "I'm happy with my present supplier," "We have all we need," and so on.

Then, think of responses you can use to get the person talking.

Write these out. Practice them. The key word here is practice.

You need to be comfortable with your response so that the instant you get resistance, you're able to quickly react.

You won't win them all, but at least you give yourself a chance.

YOUR ACTION STEPS

What will you commit to DO as a result of this section?

11 Case Study Of A Call

L et's tie everything together and look at a case study of a call submitted by a reader of my newsletter.

The Details

Art,

I am selling advertising space on the Internet and the name we are using is LocalTraders. The initial objection I quite often hear is "I am not interested." The replies we have used are,

"Not interested in what?"
"That's not an unusual reaction, however what we are offering..."

"Many of our current clients have had that initial reaction however after realizing what we have to offer changed their minds . . ."

"You're obviously very busy so I'll call back later at a more convenient time, which would suit you better, Monday or Tuesday?"

Have you any ideas to overcome "Not interested?"

I have included the script so that you can have an idea where I am coming from.

I look forward to your comments

Kindest Regards,
Doug Aird

Here is what Doug had sent.

The Script/Call Guide

With the Assistant

First: *"I hope you could help me so I'm better prepared to speak to Mr. Big, there's probably some information you could provide me with."*

"How long have you been in business?"
"Do you deal with the general public?"

"What exactly are the services you offer?"

"Would Mr. Big be interested in getting more business?"

"When would be the best time to contact Mr. Big?"

Voice Mail Message

"This is _____ from LocalTraders I might have something which may increase your business. Please contact me . . ."

Opening Statement

"Hi _____, my name is _____ and I'm from LocalTraders. Depending on your current situation I might have something that could possibly increase your business. I don't want to waste your time so do you mind if I just ask you a few simple questions to see if you may benefit?"

Questioning

"Do you deal with the general public?"

"What exactly are the services you offer?"

"Would you be interested in getting more business?"

"Are you currently advertising? How much does that cost you?"

"What are you doing online to get new business?"

"Are you aware of how others in your business are showing success online?"

"Would you be interested in being part of that growth on the internet?"

"Do you support your local community?"

> *"Do you have your own web page or are you using a common web site?"*
>
> *"If you could promote your business online for less than a bottle of Coke a week would you be interested?"*

Presentation

> *"Well, from what you have said we may be able to help you ..."*
> *"We're currently finalizing the Local Traders' site for (name of area) and we are looking for a (whatever business he is in). The site highlights and promotes local business in (area) as well as featuring local and community news and events ..."*

Art's Analysis and Recommendation

This script went on, but I had way more than enough to respond. Here's what I said:

Doug,

The best way to deal with objections is to **prevent** them. In your case, I'd strengthen the opening to make it more specific than "increase your business." That could signal to them that they are going to get hit with a sales pitch. To do this, you need to get better info before speaking with the boss.

I like the fact you are asking questions of the screener, but you also might want to include,

"How are you promoting now?"
"How do people find you?"
"How do you get new business?"
"What type of business are you looking for more of?"

Perhaps even change your prefacing remark to,

"I want to make sure that what I have would be of some interest to Mr. Bigg..." before asking questions.

Based on these answers, you could customize more of a "grabber" for each prospect.

For example,

"Ms. Prospect, I understand that you do some promotions now to generate store traffic, and advertise some 'loss leader' items to get people in the store. I have an option that might be worth considering to help you reach prospective buyers you might not be getting now, therefore getting you even more traffic."

As for some of those objections, it's typically too late to try to turn them around when you hear them, since the damage has been done. They're in a negative, nonreceptive frame of mind. And all of those rebuttals you mentioned typically serve to just harden their defenses. I believe the least-damaging course of action is to simply ask a question to take their mind off their resistance:

"I see. How do you advertise now?"

Granted, you're ignoring the resistance, and if you can get them talking, now you're at the point of the call where you want to be anyway. If they still say they're not interested, move on.

Art

(NOTE: Here is the message received back from Doug just a few days after sending him these recommendations.)

Art,

Thank you for the time you took to give some suggestions re my script, it certainly has worked!!

And all in a few short days. I have only been using the script for two days and have not had rejection. The closest I came to that was when one prospect told me he didn't want to advertise because he might be taking business away from his existing clients. I then asked who they were and he told me, one I already had the second I didn't. I called the second one and signed him up over the telephone. I'm having much more success while making fewer calls.

Kindest Regards,
Doug Aird

12 How To Get And Stay Motivated When Calling

You've experienced it. I have too. A slump, a rut . . . one of those "Everything/everyone is dumping on me," attitudes.

The key to success when placing sales and prospecting calls is how you deal with it, and not staying IN it. How you get and keep yourself motivated. That's right, I said how you motivate yourself.

No one can motivate you. Just like no one can stress you out, or reject you, you alone can allow yourself to be affected by outside influences. Therefore it's critical—especially in this profession—that you have a never-ending plan that keeps your outlook—and correspondingly, your performance—at sky-high levels. And there's one proven way to do that consistently.

Goals.

Everything of significance that you've ever achieved was likely first visualized by you as a goal. Great stuff just doesn't automatically happen.

To get more motivated, and stay that way, you need targets to shoot for. Here are tips for setting and reaching your goals, and staying motivated.

Pick goals that you desire passionately. If you just mildly wish for something, you won't muster the drive to pursue it, and weather the storms you'll encounter along the way. For example, if you just *wouldn't mind* dropping a few pounds, that's not strong enough. If you feel you *must* lose 15 pounds because you absolutely refuse to go up another clothes size, and you've had it with feeling sluggish all the time, you'll do what it will take to shed the excess baggage.

Pick goals you can see yourself attaining. Before you begin, you must be able to visualize the end result. Otherwise your subconscious will never buy into the notion you can accomplish it. People never rise above their own self-perception. If you can't see yourself earning $20,000 more than you do today, you'll never get there. Conversely, if you visualize yourself already there, you'll think of what you'll need to do to actually reach your destination.

Pick goals you're willing to work hard to achieve. Everyone would *like* to make more money. A small percentage are willing to do what it takes to make it a reality. That's part of the reason lotteries are so popular. Whatever you select as a goal has trade-offs attached. Only if you're willing to toil and sacrifice will you reach that goal.

When setting your goals, remove your doubts. Most of us fly way too close to the ground. Doubts are not the result of rational thinking, but habitual thinking. Write out some of the self-limiting beliefs that are like lead weights strapped to your feet, and rewrite them in a positive, possibility-thinking way. For example, *"I've never been able to close the large accounts where the big commissions are,"* could become, *"What I need to do is analyze what other people do who consistently close the large accounts, and work up my own strategy."*

Take risks. Sure it's a bit spooky treading into territory you've never traveled, but it's also motivating! Plus, the only risks that aren't a bit scary are the ones you've outgrown.

Don't let details get in your way. Fussing about the details burdens your thinking and fuels the fires of doubt. After setting your goal, immediately fire your machine in motion. It's easier to view the possibilities when you're moving, plus it eliminates worry. Don't worry about what happens in the middle of a jump—focus on the end.

More Motivational Tips

Recall your most motivated moments. When were you last fired up, storming toward something you desired with the intensity of an out-of-control freight train thundering down a mountain? What were you pursuing? This gives you a clue to what you really want. Can you—and are you willing—to repeat the desire and the tactics again?

Expect to excel. Ask winners and they'll tell you, matter of factly, that there was never a doubt that they'd achieve their lofty levels. Sure, they ran into road blocks along the way, but progress has a way of masquerading as problems, and they prodded along.

Act as if you've already achieved your goal. I asked a superstar rep to what he attributed his success, and he told me his life changed when he started acting like a top performer, even before he got there. He studied the people who pulled down the big numbers (and dollars), and copied their behavior . . . coming in early, not squandering phone time, asking for commitment more often . . . expecting to do well. The results followed.

Walk 25% faster. Don't laugh. Psychologists have proven body posture and movement affects attitudes. Ever see a slovenly loser walk with a spring in his step, like he actually had something important to do? No, they shuffle along. Conversely, watch the gait of achievers you admire. Their confident stride says, "I'm coming from something I just achieved, marching over to conquer another challenge."

Think "Action, Now." Rid from your vocabulary the words, "tomorrow," "later," "one of these days," "someday," and other wish-oriented vague terminology that typically results in "never"-type of behavior. Any time you're tempted to lazily shove an achievement-oriented task out to the ambiguous horizon, stop yourself and take action, immediately.

Ideas to Get You Going Now

Keep in mind that the large prospect you're waiting to call is buying from someone, but will eventually change. It might as well be from you!

To beat call reluctance, think of all the successes you've had when you dug in your heels and took action. Nothing but guilt and regret results from wasting time, avoiding the phone. Pick it up now, and equate action with accomplishment!

Set short-term activity goals, such as number of prospecting calls in a two-hour period. It keeps you focused, active, and invigorated.

Rejection is not an experience. It's how some people *define* an experience. You'll never be rejected again if you can pinpoint something positive that comes from every call.

Don't settle for "good enough." That's defined as just enough to get by and survive. Always put in that little extra.

Use Sports Psychology to Bust Out of a Slump

Ever get in one of those funks where nothing seems to be falling your way? You have deals collapse, buyers not returning calls or emails, and suddenly you're struggling to put up results.

And then, your confidence takes a hit. We question why we're not having success. Self-doubt creeps in. Maybe even to the point of not going after key accounts or avoiding calls altogether.

A *Wall Street Journal* article discussed how that happened to Dan DiCio, a high-tech equipment account exec. He was expecting to have a big year, but his results were just not there. So he began grinding . . . working longer hours, nights and weekends. To no avail.

He was grasping for a solution. What could he do to get out of this slump? Well, Dan is a big baseball fan, and he recalled how John Smoltz, a pitcher for the Atlanta Braves, in 1991, worked with a sports psychologist to pull himself out of slump. So Dan did the same thing, with tremendous results.

First, Smoltz's story: the pitcher—one of the top stars in the game at the time—started the season with a horrible record of just 2 wins and 11 losses. He said he lost his confidence. As many people do, in sales and sports, he tried working harder to get out of the slump. Instead, he made it worse, rushing himself on the mound and overanalyzing every bad pitch.

The psychologist worked with him to recover quickly from bad pitches, instead of dwelling on them. The doctor made a video of perfect pitches Smoltz had thrown and had him watch the video over and over. Then, if Smoltz threw a bad pitch in a game, he said, "I literally would not step back on the mound until I had pulled up that positive file in my mind." This reminded him of what it felt like to throw well, instilling confidence, resulting in more positive performance.

Dan's psychologist suggested the same thing: Stop overworking and relax. Recall past positive performances. The result? His 2010 sales were double the previous year's.

You Can Use the Same Techniques

You likely won't need to see a sports psychologist if you get in one of these ruts. But you can apply the same principles they teach to show similar success.

Tim Stowell, a 25-year commercial real estate broker began losing his self-confidence during the recession because of all the no's he was getting. So he implemented a technique that golfer Jack Nicklaus used to fend off anxiety. He began visualizing himself performing well. If he performs poorly during a presentation, instead of dwelling on it, he laughs it off, and refocuses on his goal of helping clients save money. Focusing on the positive helped him land more new clients.

Here are other techniques sports psychologists use with athletes, and their business clients:

- maintain an archive of recordings of good calls, or parts of calls. Listen to them on a regular basis, especially when doubt surfaces.

- list your strengths on a card and post it in front of you. For example, "Great at building rapport. Excellent product knowledge. Pleasing phone voice. Fine negotiator." Many baseball players do this with laminated cards and review them between innings.

- use relaxation techniques. You'll often see a golfer or football kicker take a deep breath before a shot, or a field goal attempt.

- after a blown call, immediately focus on a past success, and/or something good you could take out of that call. Don't dwell on the negative. Former football quarterback, Troy Aikman, said that quarterbacks need to have poor memories because they can't let a dropped pass or a missed block affect their performance on the next play. Move on. I personally teach the use of the Secondary Objective of the call, which is defined as, "What can I attempt, at minimum, on every call?" This ensures you get a win of sorts on every call.

- simplify things. In today's constantly-connected, multi-tasking environment, most people are busier than ever, but accomplishing less. When you are calling, do nothing but that for blocks of time. Focus, relax, and let it flow.

There are many similarities between athletes and sales professionals executing our performances confidently and consistently. It's human nature that with the inevitable undesired outcomes we often experience that our self esteem can be rattled. Therefore it is essential that we be proactive to battle these negative feelings and prevent them from becoming fatal. Use these techniques and you'll see your attitude and sales results at the high level you desire.

13 Top Calling Tips

For the past 33+ years of publishing my monthly sales tips newsletter, readers have consistently told me that the feature they like to read first is the back page. It's there where we share about six brief tips. Here are a selection of these profitable tips for you.

Ask the Tough Question

You're not going to sell them all. (No kidding, right?) Therefore it's in your best interest to know when to move on and cut your losses. With someone who is asking for more than you can give, you need to find out if they really want to do business with you, or are just a "vendor hopper," someone who buys from whomever offers the lowest price this month.

Ask them a tough question,

> *"Pat, it appears we have exactly what you want. Except my best price is $4.58 a unit and you're asking for $3.99. Is there a way to work this out, or should we end the conversation?"*

Sure it sounds tough, but if they're serious, they'll let you know.

Question the Lower Competitive Price

When some reps hear a prospect or customer mention a lower competitive price, they tense up and believe they have to match it to get or retain the business. A smart approach is to remain calm and question the competitive offer in order to blow holes in it. For example,

> *"Oh, that sounds like a really low price. What accessories do you receive with that? How long is the warranty?"*

Especially question in the areas where you know you are strong and offer more.

Get Off of Price and On to Value

To get a prospect/customer off a price issue and on to a value one, ask them,

> *"Let's jump ahead here. One year from now, how will you know if you made the right choice?"*

"What results do you expect from the system you choose?"
"What will change as a result of the decision you make?"

Assume They Have the Problem and Ask About It

Here's the assumptive problem questioning technique:

"Many of my clients are experiencing a lack of quality applicants responding to their recruitment ads. What is your experience?"

It's easier for someone to react to a scenario you've created than to have to think of an answer themselves. For example, *"What are your recruitment needs?"*

Don't Cave in To Get the Deal

Seems like the 80/20 rule applies to most everything. Including negotiating. Negotiation experts say that 80% of the concessions occur in the final 20% of discussions. What's important for us is that we don't appear too eager—or desperate—to get a sale, therefore caving in to concessions toward the end.

Check Press Releases to Find Contact Names

Sometimes you run into the tough, secretive switchboard operator who acts as if she works for the CIA, not allowed to provide any names or information. One alternative provided by Heather

Beck with Acterna, is looking at the press releases on a company's website. Granted, you might be fishing in a fairly empty pond, but you just might land a key name that could help you. She said that more than once she was unable to get a contact name from an operator or anywhere else on a website, but found someone quoted in a press release that she was able to call and ask for. This person normally isn't the buyer, but at least it's a start in the investigation and navigation process.

Handling the Budget Objection

When you hear the objection, "We don't have the budget," you need to first determine if that's real or a blow off.

> *"If budget weren't an issue, are we the ones you'd want?"*
> *"OK, but this is what you still want to do, right?"*
> *"If you did have the money, you'd move forward?"*

If they answer positively, then it's a matter of getting them to think creatively.

> *"How can we get the money?"*
> *"What's the best way to find the money?"*
> *"How have you handled it in the past when you needed to find funds for something you needed?"*
> *"What are some possible ways to solve this?"*

Listen to Their On-Hold Message

When you're placed on hold, pay attention to their on-hold announcements. You might hear some useful information about the company, products, or promotions.

Get Them Talking

Upon hearing an objection a tendency for some sales reps is to tense up and turn on the verbal waterfall to overcome the objection. Take the opposite approach. Get them talking.

> *"What do you suggest?"*
> *"What is the alternative?"*
> *"What will happen if you do nothing?"*
> *"What are the implications of not taking action?"*

Granted, as with most suggestions, this might not be appropriate in all situations. Pick and choose your spots.

"What's This in Reference To?"

Here's a common question from assistants: "What's this in reference to?" To give the best answer you might want to ask a question or two of your own first.

> *"Well, let me first ask you, does Mr. Ryan get involved in the credit card processing for your stores? Good. Well, depending*

on how satisfied he is with his online transactions and the fees he's paying, we might have a few options to speed up transaction time and cut down on extra charges. I'd like to ask him a few questions..."

Mute Tips

If you use the mute button for more than a few seconds, be sure to give some feedback such as "uh-hmm" the instant you get back on the phone. This way they know you're still there. By the way, use the mute sparingly, coughs, clearing of the throat . . . not so you can hold a conversation with your neighbor.

React, But Don't Reply

When you hear something that you detect is a brush off, use a vague or non-committal word or phrase.

"That's interesting."
"OK."
"That's a thought."
"Uh-huh."

If it is a real concern and you ignore it, you can be assured they'll bring it up again.

If You're Going to Get a No, Get it Today

Far too many sales reps clog up their follow-up files like a Los Angeles freeway during rush hour, with prospects who can't or won't make a decision. It's better to get some decision, rather than let them rust. John Fuhrman of Universal Underwriters is quoted in "SELLING" about what he did as a sales manager at a car dealership: he made an offbeat proposal, offering $50 to the salesperson who got a firm no from the greatest number of pending prospects. The result was exactly as he suspected. The sales force ended up making 12 appointments and selling eight cars. All from people who were pending, and were asked to make a decision.

Don't Manufacture Objections

Many objections aren't even present until the salesperson brings them up. This happens when the rep talks too much about features that are of no interest to the listener. When a salesperson drones on about what he thinks is a selling point, it may very well distract the listener from what he's really interested in—if anything—and draw attention to what he might interpret as a liability. Don't talk too much, and only present what they're interested in. A benefit is only a benefit if the person hearing it perceives it to be a benefit at that very instant.

I Want to Talk it Over

When someone tells you they are going to talk it over with another person or committee, respond with,

> *"Can I interpret that as a definite sign of interest on your part?"*

Or try a stronger question such as,

> *"Are you going to be recommending it to them when you do talk it over?"*

Don't get off the phone until you know the answers to these questions. They could be stalling, which means you're wasting your valuable time by calling back. If they truly are interested, you can find that out and help them sell it to the other person.

Ways to Begin Questions

The way you word your questions has a huge impact on the quality and quantity of information you get in return. Here are some good ways to begin questions.

> *"Please describe..."*
> *"Please explain..."*
> *"Compare for me how you..."*
> *"To what extent...?"*
> *"In what way do you...?"*

"Give me an idea of how..."
"What is the process for...?"
"Go through the..."

The Truth About Scripting

Let me be clear on this: You DO need to, and will sound better when you prepare what you will say, before you say it live.

Any time I hear or read a sales trainer, manager, or a rep demean the use of sales scripts, they lose credibility with me. Sometimes the problem is in their definition and perception of a sales script, which usually has more to do with the delivery, such as reading something in a monotone voice.

In that case, I agree. Kids like to be read to, adults don't.

I suggest you look at a script like an actor, and deliver it the same way. Otherwise, "winging it" and generally being unprepared usually yields horrible results.

It's actually kind of a contradiction. Many people who don't like scripts feel that way because they say scripts cause a person to sound like a doofus.

Well, what happens when someone gets on a call, unprepared, rambles, stutters and stammers. Yup, doofus.

Really. If you are able to prepare for what you'll say, and then edit, practice, and fine-tune it, why wouldn't you?

You wouldn't turn in a rough draft if you were going to write a very high-profile article in your industry publication would you? But a rough draft is precisely what you deliver when you aren't totally prepared on calls.

Every day, salespeople insist on diving blindly into calls, and puking all over themselves with the first words that come to mind.

Would a surgeon walk into an operating room, slap on the gloves and say, "OK, give me the knife. By the way, what are we doing with this guy?"

Would a lawyer dash into a trial, pop open a briefcase, begin an opening argument, then turn and whisper to the client, "What are we working on here again?"

In either case, I hope not.

In my inside sales training and cold call training programs, we work on how to craft the persuasive, natural-sounding script that is easy to deliver, and gets results. Then reps must be prepared to deliver it at the right moment.

Let's grade your level of preparedness as of right now in each of these areas.

Screeners and Assistants
Can you instantly provide a response to the question, "What is this in reference to?" And I mean a good, results-oriented answer, not one that gets you screened out.

Opening Statements and Voice Mail
These most certainly need to be prepared, word-for-word.

Early Resistance
We covered this a few chapters ago . . . hearing "I'm not interested" at the beginning of a call. When you are prepared, you can engage them in conversation and move them to a state of interest and curiosity.

Unexpected Answers to Questions
We're all able to build sales momentum when they follow the script we'd like . . . answering questions with the positive, interest-filled responses that lead to our objective. But what about the ones we DON'T want? The ones that resemble a hard-drive crash, wiping away all of your memory.

Real Objections
Here we must be prepared with questions you created in that chapter.

In each of these areas, I recommend the same prescription for excellence: work and preparation.

There's no easy way to sound smooth.

A sales rep told me at a recent training seminar, "You make it look so easy, coming up with quick answers. How do you do it?"

Oh, it was easy, I told him. After over 33 years, over 1700 sales training presentations, thousands of sales calls, and thousands of hours of writing, reading, and practicing, it just comes naturally.

C'mon, no one is naturally smooth. Although almost everyone can sound that way. But we must be un-smooth and uncomfortable first. Before you can golf in the 80's, you go through the 90's.

If you want to raise yourself to the next level, go back to the basics and beyond.

ACTION STEPS

Lock yourself in a room with a pad of paper. Begin by writing out the headings above, and any other difficult situations you encounter. Review our chapters in each of these areas.

Then, stretch, knead, and rack your mind until you create word-for-word statements, responses and questions you're comfortable with.

Then, go to the next level. Like a military strategist preparing for all possible scenarios, brainstorm for their possible responses. Keep repeating the process. Then practice it out loud. Role play with a partner.

Recite—don't read—into a recorder.

What's great about this is that the more you practice, the better you become, which means better results. Which means you have more fun on calls.

Which also means you're more confident.

And people will be saying about you, "You sound so smooth! You're a natural." Thanks to your scripts.

Final Words . . .

In my over 33 years of helping professionals say and do the right thngs to get more business by phone, I've unfortunately heard my share of words like these.

"I've been through training before."
"I've seen that stuff before."
"I've been in sales quite a while."
"I do pretty good."

Let me put it in another light. What if you heard the following?

From a Cardiac Surgeon: "I had a class on heart surgery once back in medical school. That's good enough."

From a Professional Baseball Player: "I don't need to go to Spring Training, or take batting practice or infield before games. I've been playing for a number of years."

From an Olympic Figure Skater: "I practiced a routine once, a few years ago. I don't need to go through it again before competition."

Fat Guy at the Pizza Buffet: "I am in shape. I own a treadmill and even used it once."

Of course, those are all absurd statements. As are the ones from sales reps and managers who think they, or their people are good enough.

The fact is, "good enough" does not win championships, or make people excellent or wealthy. (And by the way, sales managers who think that experience alone makes for a good salesperson, think again. Experience measures **attendance**. *Accomplishment and results* measures success, and continued learning ensures it.)

So, what's my point?

You likely have not come close to reaching your potential as a sales professional.

Few people have.

I know I haven't.

In order to accomplish more of what you're capable of, I challenge you to look at your own "good enough" barrier and break through it, regardless of how high that bar is for you.

This invisible obstacle is what holds many people back. Just when people begin approaching an opportunity to put in a little extra, to invest in themselves, to seize a potential new achievement, many hit this mental boundary and say to themselves, "That's good enough."

Good enough is when talented people don't fully develop their abilities.

Good enough is when service slips and customers complain.

Good enough is when sales professionals do what it takes to get by, but miss growth and income opportunities in the process.

People who are satisfied with Good Enough cheat themselves, their family, their company, and their customers.

Action Step: If you're serious about sales as a career—not just something you do to pay the bills—take a serious look at what you're doing to improve your "sales health."

Like I always say, sales is an art, a science, and a skill. It takes continual digestion and implementation of new information, and practicing in order to reach new levels.

Just when you're about to say, "This is good enough," push that barrier away.

Go that extra inch.

Health experts suggest exercising 20-30 minutes at a time, 3-5 times per week.

If you invested an equal amount of time on your sales health . . . reading, listening to audios, watching videos, and even writing, you can accomplish things other people—with low Good Enough barometers—will never come close to reaching.

I encourage and challenge you to be the best salesperson you can be, and use the phone to its fullest potential.

Certainly use the ideas we went through together in this book.

If you haven't already, be sure you get my free weekly Smart Calling Tips and YouTube training videos. **BusinessByPhone.com/free-stuff**

Visit my blog for tons of other tips and best practices: **SmartCalling.com**

Shop for the training resource that is just right for you, whether it be audio, video, books, or complete training programs. **BusinessByPhone.com/shop**

If you are really serious about your sales success and want to go to the next level, enroll in my Smart Calling College training. **SmartCallingCollege.com**

Best yet: have a customized training program developed for your company or association, delivered at your location or venue of your choice. **BusinessByPhone.com/hire-art**, or call me at 800-326-7721.

I look forward to helping you reach your sales and income goals and dreams.